THE

SIMPLE LIFE

DEVOTIONAL THOUGHTS
FROM AMISH COUNTRY

THE
SIMPLE LIFE

DEVOTIONAL THOUGHTS
FROM AMISH COUNTRY

WANDA E.
BRUNSTETTER

BARBOUR
PUBLISHING

Published by Barbour Publishing, Inc., P.O. Box 719, Uhrichsville, Ohio 44683, www.barbourbooks.com

Our mission is to publish and distribute inspirational products offering exceptional value and biblical encouragement to the masses.

ECPA Member of the
Evangelical Christian
Publishers Association

Printed in India.

To all my Amish friends
who have helped me gain
a better understanding of the simple life.

Contents

INTRODUCTION

Have you ever felt like your life is too busy? Have you ever stressed over *things*—feeling the pressure to "keep up with the Joneses" or perhaps wanting instead to downsize and be rid of the clutter? Have you ever imagined a simpler life, full of the blessings of family, friends, and faith?

Who hasn't?

It's for everyone who has longed for a less stressful, more peaceful existence that *The Simple Life* was written. Based on stories of our Amish friends, these sixty devotionals provide practical and thought-provoking ideas on living a more satisfying life.

The Amish are a group of people who, due to the religious persecution they suffered in Europe, relocated to America in the early 1700s. There are now more than 130,000 Amish living in various communities throughout the United States and Canada.

Their interpretation of scripture leads the Amish to live simply, without many of the modern conveniences the "English" (non-Amish) people take for granted—things like automobiles, electricity, and other helpful technologies. Dressing plainly, helping neighbors, cooking for one's family, pulling weeds in the garden—these common experiences of the Amish are often foreign to our fast-paced modern society.

Many "English" people desire a slower-paced life, which allows more time with family and friends and spends less of itself on possessions. As an author of Amish novels, I often hear comments from readers expressing a wish to slow down and live a more simple life.

Perhaps we can learn a few lessons from the Amish. Yet one need not wear plain clothes or drive a horse and buggy to find a simpler life. Quietness and peacefulness are really a matter of the heart.

Within the pages of this book, you will find sixty true-to-life Amish stories accompanied by inspirational thoughts—you'll even find some delicious recipes popular with the Amish! It is my hope that each reading will give you an intriguing glimpse into the Amish culture—but more importantly, help you discover a sense of peace and joy and a desire to live life a little more simply. . .and a little closer to God.

WANDA E. BRUNSTETTER

FRIENDLY WELCOME

Be not forgetful to entertain strangers:
for thereby some have entertained angels unawares.
HEBREWS 13:2

Are you sure your Amish friends won't mind us stopping by?" Rick asked Wayne as they drove onto a graveled driveway.

Rick's wife, Eileen, nodded. "We feel funny about dropping in unannounced."

Wayne turned off the car's engine. "I've known Eli for some time. I'm sure he and Joanna will be pleased to meet our friends."

"Joanna and Eli have always been hospitable to me," Wayne's wife, Karen, added.

As they left the car and strolled past an Amish buggy parked near the barn, Eileen's apprehension rose. Would this Amish couple really welcome people they had never met?

When they entered the expansive yard, Eileen noticed two children romping in the nearby creek. The tow-headed boy's dark trousers were rolled to the knees, and blue cotton shirttails peeked around tan suspenders. The little girl didn't seem to care that the hem of her long blue dress was getting wet, while she giggled and flicked water with her bare toes.

A young Amish woman wearing a dark green dress with a black cape and apron stepped out the back door. A tall Amish man with reddish blond hair and matching beard followed. Wayne made the introductions, explaining that Rick and Eileen were visiting from the state of Washington.

"Welcome," Joanna said, motioning to the picnic table. "Would you care to sit awhile?"

"Maybe you'd like a glass of iced tea," Eli offered with a friendly grin.

For the next hour, the three couples sat at the picnic table, visiting, watching the children play, and savoring the pleasant taste of cool mint tea.

When it was time to go, Eileen shook Joanna's hand and said, "Thank you for your hospitality. We've enjoyed our visit."

"You're welcome," Joanna replied.

As they drove away, Eileen reflected on their time spent with the Amish family. She felt like they had made some new friends. *Would I have been as pleasant and hospitable if uninvited guests had showed up at my house? How many times have I put off writing a letter or phoning a friend because I was too busy? When was the last time I entertained strangers?*

Hospitality seems easier when we are with family and friends, but God reminds us to entertain those outside our familiar circle. In Mark 9:41, we are reminded that Jesus said, "For whosoever shall give you a cup of water to drink in my name, because ye belong to Christ, verily I say unto you, he shall not lose his reward." Whether it be a cup of water or a glass of iced tea, God is pleased when we show hospitality. After all, for some people, our friendship and hospitality may be the only Jesus they will ever see.

FOOD FOR THOUGHT

Good friends are like good quilts;
they never lose their warmth.

FOOD FOR THE BODY

Mint Tea
Ingredients:
    2 quarts fresh mint leaves
    1 cup sugar
    Boiling water

Fill a large kettle with fresh, clean mint leaves, add sugar, and cover with boiling water. Stir until sugar is dissolved. Cover and let stand several hours or overnight. Remove mint leaves by straining. Then pour the remaining cooled tea into a pitcher to refrigerate or serve later in ice-filled glasses.

KATHRYN B.

No Sales Pitch Needed

Let your light so shine before men,
that they may see your good works,
and glorify your Father which is in heaven.
MATTHEW 5:16

Danki [thank you] for helping me with the pie stand today," Emma said to her teenage sons, Adam and Joseph.

"*Du bischt willkumm* [you are welcome]." Adam wiggled his dark eyebrows. "Everything looks good, and I may eat a whole pie myself if we don't sell them all."

"We'd better do what we can to be sure they sell." Joseph poked his brother playfully. "Mom's gone to a lot of work baking all these goodies."

Emma clicked her tongue. "We don't want to do a sales pitch when folks stop by. The best way is to let the baked goods sell themselves."

"*Jah,* that's right," Adam agreed. "If the pies look good, then people will buy."

A short time later, a van pulled up, and two English women got out.

"I hear that the Amish make some real tasty pies," one of the women commented as they approached the stand.

"It's a nice day, isn't it?" Emma asked with a smile, making no reference to her pies.

"It certainly is," the second English woman agreed.

"You're welcome to look around," Joseph said. "And if you have any questions, feel free to ask."

The first woman smiled. "All of the pies look wonderful. I'm sure any of them would be good."

Emma nodded. "I hope so."

"Do you have any shoofly pie?" the other woman questioned. "That's my favorite kind."

"Right over there." Adam pointed to the left side of the stand.

The woman picked up two pies and brought them over to the battery-operated cash register where Emma stood. "I'll take these."

"I'm going to get an apple-crumb pie," the other woman said.

A short time later, as the women walked back to their van, one of them said, "It's nice to buy something without getting a sales pitch."

Emma smiled at her boys, knowing they'd heard it, too. They'd made the right choice, letting the quality of the product do all the selling that was needed.

Often we feel frustrated when someone gives us a sales pitch. We become wary and doubtful of what they're saying. It can be the same when we talk about our faith. We should avoid trying to "sell" someone on Jesus. Instead, by allowing people to see God's light and love in us, they will be more apt to come to Him. Let the work He's doing in our lives do the talking.

In John 13:35, Jesus told His disciples the following: "By this shall all men know that ye are my disciples, if ye have love one to another."

May others know we belong to Jesus by the love they see in us.

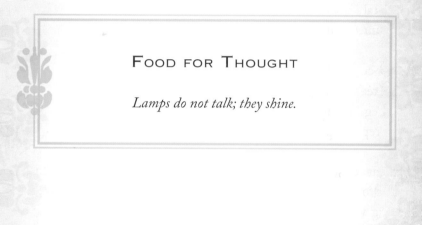

FOOD FOR THOUGHT

Lamps do not talk; they shine.

Shoofly Pie

Ingredients:

- 1 cup flour
- ⅔ cup brown sugar
- 1 tablespoon butter, crumbled
- 1 cup light molasses (or ½ cup dark molasses and ½ cup Karo syrup)
- ¾ cup boiling water
- 1 teaspoon baking soda
- 1 egg, beaten
- Prepared pie shell

Preheat oven to 375 degrees. Mix the flour, brown sugar, and butter together in a small bowl. In another bowl, mix the molasses, boiling water, baking soda, and beaten egg. Add half the crumb mixture to the liquid mixture, but do not beat. Pour into the prepared pie shell and cover the top with the remaining crumbs. Bake for 10 minutes, then lower oven temperature to 350 degrees. Bake for another 30 minutes. May be served as a breakfast pie or as dessert.

MIRIAM B.

ANSWERED PRAYERS

It shall come to pass, that before they call,
I will answer;
and while they are yet speaking,
I will hear.

ISAIAH 65:24

A thunderous roar pelted the ground outside of Rebekah and Samuel's bedroom window, and they bolted upright in bed. *"Was in der welt* [what in all the world]*?"* Rebekah exclaimed. "What is that horrible noise?"

Samuel scrambled out of bed and rushed to the window. "It's the mules! They've gotten out of the barn."

Rebekah grabbed her robe from a wall peg, and Samuel stepped into his trousers, pulling his suspenders over his shoulders. There was no time for further discussion. They needed to act fast. If the mules made their way to the road, a car might hit them. If they trampled the vegetable garden or the cornstalks in the field, everything would be ruined.

Samuel rushed out the back door, and Rebekah stepped into the cool night air behind him. She paused and offered a silent prayer. *Dear Lord, please help us get the mules back to the barn.*

A few minutes later, Rebekah turned the corner of the house and was surprised to see Samuel heading for the barn with ten draft mules obediently following. She breathed a prayer of thanks as she helped him secure the mules inside their respective stalls.

"I'm surprised at how easily you led them in," she said.

Samuel nodded. "As soon as I left the house I began praying that the mules would cooperate."

"I was praying that, too."

Samuel smiled. "I know there are times when we must wait for God's reply, but it never ceases to amaze me when He responds quickly to our prayers."

She nodded. "I think sometimes, even before we ask, the Lord answers our prayers."

One of the reasons people pray is out of a sense of need. Sometimes, however, we forget to pray and instead try to take matters into our own hands. Even though God knows our needs before we ask, He wants us to seek His help. He may answer quickly or make us wait, but we can be sure that He will answer, according to His will.

In 1 John 5:14, we are reminded: "And this is the confidence that we have in him, that, if we ask any thing according to his will, he heareth us."

May we always remember to call on God whenever we have a need.

FOOD FOR THOUGHT

*If you are too busy to pray,
you are busier than God wants you to be.*

FOOD FOR THE BODY

Cornmeal Muffins
Ingredients:
    1½ cups cornmeal
    1½ cups flour
    1 teaspoon baking powder
    1 teaspoon salt
    1 tablespoon butter
    ½ teaspoon sugar
    2 eggs
    Milk

Preheat oven to 350 degrees. Mix the above ingredients together in a large bowl and add enough milk to make a stiff batter. Spoon into greased muffin tins. Bake 25–30 minutes. Serve warm. Delicious with honey.

MATTIE STOLTZFUS

LEND A HAND

Bear ye one another's burdens,
and so fulfil the law of Christ.
GALATIANS 6:2

As Edith and her teenage daughter, Stella, left the auction and headed across the parking lot, they were shocked to discover their buggy horse straddling the hitching rail, neighing and thrashing about. He'd obviously tried to break free, and the front of the buggy was now pushed up against his back legs, leaving the horse in a precarious position.

"I'll pull and you push," Edith told Stella. "We've got to get our horse off the rail before he gets hurt!"

After several tries, Edith felt so worn out from trying to free their frantic horse that she was ready to give up. It was obvious that she and Stella couldn't accomplish the task alone.

About that time, several English people showed up, offering their assistance. One man had a rope, which he put around the horse's neck. Two other men got behind the animal, and as they pushed, the first man tugged on the rope.

The horse continued to struggle but finally broke free from the railing and fell to the ground. He lay there awhile, wheezing and thrashing. Then, slowly he rose to his feet, a bit wobbly but apparently unharmed.

"Thank you so much," Edith told the men who had helped. "We couldn't do this by ourselves."

"I'm glad your horse is okay," one man replied.

Edith nodded, grateful that strangers had been willing to help in her time of need.

How often do we get busy and fail to see the needs of others? Have you ever witnessed someone in need and done nothing about it? Have you ever been the one in need but received no help?

In Isaiah 41:6, we are told: "They helped every one his neighbor; and every one said to his brother, Be of good courage." Not only are we blessed when someone bears our burdens, but the one who has helped is blessed.

FOOD FOR THOUGHT

Timely good deeds are nicer than afterthoughts.

FOOD FOR THE BODY

Bread and Butter Pickles
Ingredients:
- 25–30 cucumbers, medium, sliced thin
- 8 white onions, large, chopped
- ½ cup salt
- 2 cups cider vinegar
- 5 cups sugar
- 3 cups water
- ½ teaspoon cloves
- 2 tablespoons mustard seeds
- 1 teaspoon turmeric

Combine cucumbers, onions, and salt in a large bowl. Let stand for 3 hours. Drain. Combine vinegar, sugar, water, and spices in a large kettle; bring to a boil. Add cucumber mixture. Heat thoroughly, but do not boil. Pack while hot into clean, sterilized jars and seal at once.

SARAH MILLER

A DOUBLE TREAT

A patient man has great understanding,
but a quick-tempered man displays folly.
PROVERBS 14:29 NIV

Heavenly Father," Irma prayed, staring out the window at the snow-covered schoolyard, "please give me the wisdom to know how to deal with my unruly students."

This was Irma's first year of teaching at the one-room school-house, and the last few months had been difficult. Many of the children acted as if they wanted to be in control. Others seemed insecure and unwilling to do their assignments. Some pupils were rowdy, ignoring her instructions. Irma had lectured, punished, and threatened to tell the children's parents if things didn't change. So far, nothing had worked.

When Irma heard children's laughter in the schoolyard, she drew in a deep breath and opened the front door. She stepped onto the porch just in time to see a snowball speeding her way. She ducked, but not quickly enough. The icy sphere hit her arm with a *splat*.

Irma gritted her teeth. She was certain that Michael, the boy who'd thrown the snowball, had done it on purpose. He'd been the instigator of several things in the past.

I will not let my anger get the best of me. There must be a way to deal with this. She closed the door and went to the coatroom, where she had left the wicker basket she'd brought from home. She placed it on her desk just as several noisy scholars tromped into the room.

Irma waited until the children had removed their wraps and taken their seats before she spoke. "Today we will begin class with hot chocolate and cookies," she said, removing a thermos and a plate of cookies from the basket.

Mary Alice's hand shot up. "How come?"

Irma smiled. "Because it's cold outside, and I want to let you know how special you are to me."

The room became quiet, until another hand shot up.

"Yes, Michael?"

"I think you're special, Teacher, and I'm sorry for throwing that snowball."

"I forgive you." Tears welled up in Irma's eyes. *If I had known what a little hot chocolate and some cookies could do, I would have brought them to school sooner.*

Often, when we are frustrated because things don't go our way or someone does something to upset us, we respond in anger. Scripture reminds us, however, that the best antidote for anger is prayer. "He that is slow to anger is better than the mighty; and he that ruleth his spirit than he that taketh a city" (Proverbs 16:32).

There is a time for correction, but it should never be done in anger. Many times the best lesson is learned from encouragement. Is there someone you might encourage today?

Correction does much, but encouragement does more.

FOOD FOR THE BODY

Double Treat Cookies

Ingredients:

- 2 cups sugar
- 1½ cups brown sugar
- 2 cups shortening
- 2 cups peanut butter
- 4 eggs
- 3 cups flour
- 6 cups quick-cooking oats
- 2 teaspoons vanilla
- 1 teaspoon salt
- 4 teaspoons baking soda
- 2 cups chocolate chips

Preheat oven to 400 degrees. Combine all ingredients in a large bowl. Blend by hand until ingredients are evenly and thoroughly mixed. Shape dough into balls. Place on a cookie sheet and flatten with a glass dipped in sugar. Bake 10 minutes or until done.

ESTHER RABER

No Need for Salt

*"God did this so that men would seek him
and perhaps reach out for him and find him,
though he is not far from each one of us."*
ACTS 17:27 NIV

"Can I borrow some of your salt?" eight-year-old Leroy asked his mother.

Elsie turned from her job of making potato salad and squinted at him. "Now why would you be needing my salt?"

"There's a bluebird sittin' on the porch rail, and I want to salt his tail."

"Why would you do such a thing, Leroy?"

He stared up at her with serious dark eyes. "He won't let me catch him, and my friend, Nelson, told me if you put salt on a bird's tail, it can't fly off."

Elsie clicked her tongue. "Would you really want to capture the poor thing that way?"

"I just want to make friends with the bird."

"Don't you think there's a better way than trying to keep it from flying away?"

He shrugged. "Got any idea how I might get the bluebird to stick around?"

She smiled. "Why don't you try feeding it, and see if you can gain its confidence that way?"

Leroy jumped up, pushing his chair away from the table.

"Where are you going?"

"Out to the barn to get some birdseed. I'm gonna make friends with that bird!" He paused and turned back around. "Guess I won't be needin' any of your salt after all."

It's basic human nature to want others to do things our way. Some people may try to force others to do what they want by placing unrealistic demands on them or trying to trick them into submission. Yet God never forces us to do anything against our will. His love is unconditional. He wants everyone to come willingly to Him, and He will never force us or hold us captive.

Everyone feels happier when they are allowed to do something of their own free will rather than being forced to do it. Shouldn't we give others that freedom, too?

FOOD FOR THOUGHT

The human heart, at whatever age,
opens only to the heart that opens in return.

Overnight Potato Salad
Ingredients:
    12 potatoes, medium, boiled
    12 eggs, hard-boiled
    1½ cups finely chopped celery
    1 onion, medium, chopped fine
    Salad dressing

Grate potatoes and eggs. Mix together with onion and celery, then add dressing and let set overnight.

Salad Dressing
Ingredients:
    3 cups mayonnaise or Miracle Whip
    ⅛ cup cider vinegar
    ½ cup milk
    1½ cups sugar
    6 tablespoons mustard
    3 teaspoons salt

Combine all ingredients in a bowl. Add desired amount to potato salad. Refrigerate any remaining dressing.

                                        Mrs. Jacob Stutzman

A COLORFUL PROMISE

*The L****ORD**** is my light and my salvation; whom shall I fear?*
PSALM 27:1

When Dorothy headed to her propane-operated refrigerator to get a carton of eggs, she noticed her seven-year-old son, David, standing at the window with his nose pressed against the glass. "*Guder mariye* [good morning]," she said. "Did you sleep well last night?"

"Jah, I guess." He released a sigh. "I was hopin' I could play outside today, but I see it's still rainin'."

Dorothy set the eggs on the counter and joined her son at the window. "We do need the rain to help things grow."

"But it's been raining all week." David turned to face her, and tears gathered in the corners of his eyes. "I'm scared. What if the rain keeps up and our whole yard gets flooded?"

Dorothy gathered her son into her arms. "God doesn't want us to be fearful, son. He wants us to trust Him for everything."

Just then the back door opened, and Dorothy's husband, John, entered the room. "Hey, you two. Come outside and see the pretty rainbow!"

Dorothy and David followed John out the back door.

The family stood on the lawn with their faces lifted toward the eastern sky. It had been dark and rainy the last time Dorothy looked out the kitchen window. Now the sky was a hazy blue, and a vivid rainbow made a perfect arc, twinkling radiant colors of blue, green, red, yellow, and purple.

"It's God's colorful promise that He will never again flood the whole earth," John announced.

Dorothy smiled and hugged David. "See! God takes care of us. Always. And we should remember to thank Him and not be afraid."

Everyone has some fear that's hard to release, but the Bible gives us God's answer to fear. In 2 Timothy 1:7, we are told, "For God hath not given us the spirit of fear; but of power, and of love, and of a sound mind." A simple thing such as a rainbow in the sky can remind us that God is there constantly, loving and protecting us. He will always keep His promises.

FOOD FOR THOUGHT

There's a rainbow of hope that is shining above,
reminding us of God's endless love.

FOOD FOR THE BODY

Breakfast Casserole
Ingredients:
- 6 eggs, beaten
- 2 cups milk
- 2 cups bread crumbs
- 2 cups Velveeta cheese, cubed
- ½ teaspoon salt
- ⅛ teaspoon onion salt
- 1 pound bulk sausage, browned and chilled
- Cheese slices

Combine the first seven ingredients in a large bowl, then pour into a greased cake pan. Refrigerate overnight.

Preheat oven to 350 degrees, then bake for 30 minutes or until heated through. Top with cheese slices and leave in the oven until cheese melts. Turn several times while baking.

CLARA MAST

Always Ready

Heal me, O LORD, and I shall be healed;
save me, and I shall be saved: for thou art my praise.
JEREMIAH 17:14

It was a sultry summer day, and Barbara's husband, Amos, was in the fields baling hay. Barbara had been busy in the kitchen all morning, cleaning and baking. She glanced across the room, where her infant daughter lay sleeping in her cradle. Matthew and Benjamin, ages four and six, were outside playing on the porch. "So much to do here," she said with a sigh. "And I really should help Amos with the baling."

For the next several hours, Barbara rushed from the fields to the house, helping her husband handle the bales of hay, mopping floors, and caring for the children. By evening, she was exhausted.

The following day, Barbara came down with a terrible headache. She took some aspirin, hoping she would feel better by the time they got to their friends' house, where they had been invited for supper. When they returned home, Barbara's headache was worse.

"I hope I feel better in the morning," she told Amos as they prepared for bed. "I have berries and peas to pick, plus several loads of laundry to do."

During the night, Barbara's body heated with fever. She awoke the following morning, feeling worse and knowing she couldn't do any of her chores. Thankfully, her sister showed up to help, along with Amos's brother and parents.

When Barbara's fever went higher and she was unable to get out of bed, Amos took her to the doctor. Although Barbara heard all that was being said, she could make no response or even move. She was sure any minute would be her last.

Am I ready to leave this world? she asked herself. *Am I sure that if I died right now I would go to heaven?* She whispered a silent prayer. *Lord, forgive me for any wrongs I have done. Thank You for sending Jesus to die for my sins.*

Later that day, after a shot and intravenous fluid, Barbara felt well enough to return home. The doctor said he wasn't sure of the cause of her mysterious malady, but Barbara was thankful to be alive and to have her health restored.

Although we all have responsibilities that we have to take care of, the things of this world should never be our complete focus. We should always be thankful for our good health, but we need to remember that it could be taken from us at any time. More importantly, we must be ready to meet Jesus, for no one knows what the future holds. God has promised to forgive our sins. All we have to do is ask.

"And Jesus answering said unto them, They that are whole need not a physician; but they that are sick. I came not to call the righteous, but sinners to repentance" (Luke 5:31–32).

It should be our main interest in this world to secure an interest in the next.

FOOD FOR THE BODY

Crushed Pineapple Upside-Down Cake
Ingredients:
>1 (20 ounce) can crushed pineapple
>½ cup unsalted butter
>1 cup brown sugar, firmly packed
>2 cups pastry flour, sifted
>1¾ cups sugar
>3 teaspoons baking powder
>1 teaspoon salt
>¼ cup shortening
>1 egg
>1 cup milk
>1 teaspoon vanilla

Preheat oven to 350 degrees. Grease a 9 x 9-inch pan. Combine undrained pineapple, butter, and brown sugar in a bowl. Spread on the bottom of the pan. Sift flour, sugar, baking powder, and salt in another bowl. Add the shortening, egg, milk, and vanilla. Beat well. Pour over the fruit mixture in the pan and bake for 45–50 minutes. Turn the cake upside down and eat plain or serve with whipped topping.

LIZZIE MILLER

ONE BODY

For as the body is one, and hath many members,
and all the members of that one body,
being many, are one body: so also is Christ.
1 Corinthians 12:12

As Leah stepped into the yard, carrying a platter of ham, she was greeted by the sight of more than one hundred English and Amish friends and neighbors who had come to help build her husband's barn. Everyone had been assigned a job. Henry Zook, the man with the longest beard and the most knowledge of barn raisings, stood near the construction site, telling some of the men what they should do. There were men and boys scattered around the yard, cutting wood into the proper sizes and hauling it to the location of the new building. More men stood on the crossbeams, working together in an orderly fashion, as the trusses for the barn roof came together.

"Looks like there will be plenty to eat for the noon meal," Leah's friend, Becky, said as she placed a jug of iced tea on the table.

Leah pulled her attention away from the workers and nodded. "Jah, and so many of the women in our community have come to help serve the food." She glanced around the yard, where several women rushed around, setting out platters of ham, chicken, and roast beef, as well as a variety of salads, breads, cut-up vegetables, and relishes. There was plenty of coffee, tea, and lemonade, and for dessert there were several kinds of pies, cakes, and cookies.

"Looks like things are going well on Sam's new barn," Becky

said, nodding toward the rising structure on the other side of the yard. "Those hardworking men have it half built already."

"It's amazing how much can be done when we all work together," Leah said with a smile. "Makes me glad for the help of all our friends. We are certainly one body today."

There is strength in unity, for people working together can do many things that people alone can't do. But in order for that to happen, we need to be close to one another and share life together so we can strengthen each other. This applies to the home, as well as the church.

"For the body is not one member, but many," the apostle Paul said in 1 Corinthians 12:14. Each one in the body is important, and each one has a job to do. With Christ as the head of the body, and everyone working together, we can get a lot done to further His kingdom.

FOOD FOR THOUGHT

Many hands make work seem lighter,
especially if they are proficiently skilled hands.

Shoofly Cake
Ingredients:
- 2 cups brown sugar
- ½ cup lard or shortening
- 1 egg
- 1 teaspoon baking soda
- 3 cups flour
- 1½ cups sour milk
- Crumbs

Crumbs
Ingredients:
- 1 cup flour
- 1 cup brown sugar
- 1 tablespoon lard or shortening

Preheat oven to 350 degrees. Grease a 9 x 12-inch pan. Combine first six ingredients, then pour into pan. Blend ingredients for crumb mixture, then sprinkle over top. Bake for 45–50 minutes.

Arie Elaine King

FROM THE HEART

Give, and it shall be given unto you; good measure,
pressed down, and shaken together, and running over,
shall men give into your bosom.
For with the same measure that ye mete
withal it shall be measured to you again.

LUKE 6:38

When Frieda heard a horse and buggy rumble into the yard, she was working on the ever-present weeds that were sprouting between two rows of beans. She straightened, rubbed the kinks from her back, and looked toward the drive. She was glad to see her neighbor, Wilma, step down from her buggy. It had been awhile since they'd taken the time to visit. Besides, Frieda had been pulling weeds for several hours and needed a break, so she welcomed the interruption. She left the garden and motioned Wilma over to the porch. "Can you sit awhile?"

Wilma nodded and took a seat on the porch swing. "When I pulled into the yard, I noticed you were busy in the garden. How's everything going?"

Frieda sat beside her. "Real fine. Looks like we'll have plenty of everything this year. The garden is producing nicely."

Wilma stared at her hands, clasped tightly in her lap. "Wish I could say the same for our struggling garden."

"Things aren't growing so well?"

Wilma shook her head. "That's one of the reasons I dropped by. I was hoping you might have enough corn to share a few ears."

Frieda smiled. "I have more than enough. In fact, I'd be happy to give you some green beans and beets, too."

Tears welled up in Wilma's brown eyes. "You've made me feel blessed by your willingness to share."

"I'm more than willing to give to others out of the abundance God has given me." Frieda reached for her neighbor's hand. "While you're here, would you care for a cup of tea and some freshly baked biscuits?"

"Jah, I'd like that."

Like Frieda, we should never feel that sharing what God has given us with our friends is a burden or a duty. It should be a joy. After all, Acts 20:35 reminds us, "It is more blessed to give than to receive." When we see that someone else has a need, we should be willing to help out. Yet when we have a need, we should never be too proud to ask our friends or family for help, either. Both the giver and the receiver are blessed when we share.

Great joy comes with giving to others from the bounty God has given, and He is pleased when we demonstrate such love to our friends and neighbors.

FOOD FOR THOUGHT

While seeking happiness for others,
we unconsciously find it for ourselves.

Food for the Body

Melt in Your Mouth Biscuits
Ingredients:
- 2 cups flour, sifted
- 2 teaspoons baking powder
- ½ teaspoon cream of tartar
- ½ teaspoon salt
- 2 tablespoons sugar
- ½ cup shortening
- ⅔ cup milk
- 1 egg

Preheat oven to 450 degrees. In a large bowl, sift together all dry ingredients. Cut in the shortening until the mixture is crumbly. Add milk, then egg. Blend well. Roll out the dough and cut, or drop by spoonfuls onto a baking sheet. Bake for 10–15 minutes. Very good with sausage gravy.

MIRIAM MILLER

THE WRONG NOTE

In thee, O LORD, do I put my trust: let me never be put to confusion.
PSALM 71:1

I have some mail that needs to go out," Cora said to her son, Ervin, one Monday morning. "Would you mind putting it in the mailbox for me on your way to school?"

"Sure, I can do that, Mama," Ervin replied.

She handed him two letters—one addressed to the Amish newspaper, with which she wanted to place an ad, and the other to her twin sister, Dora, who had recently moved to Illinois. "Have a good day in school, son."

A week later, when Cora went out to the road to get her mail, she was pleased to discover a letter from her twin. Anxious to see what Dora had to say, Cora hurried back to the house, poured herself a cup of tea, and took a seat at the table.

Dear Cora:

I received the strangest note from you the other day. It was a notice, advertising German shepherd puppies for sale. I think maybe it was meant for the Amish newspaper, and they must have gotten the letter you had written to me.

Dora's letter went on to tell about her family and how well they'd been getting along since their move to Illinois, but Cora could hardly focus on the words. She kept wondering what the people who worked for the newspaper must have thought when they received the letter she'd written her sister.

"Guess that's what I get for not paying attention. I was so busy the morning I wrote those letters that I got *verhuddelt* [confused] and put them in the wrong envelopes." Cora's gaze went to the Bible lying on the table, and she realized it had been several days since she had read it. She had just been too busy. She sighed. "I should never be that busy. If I don't put my trust in God, pray, and read His Word every day, I could become confused about spiritual things, too."

In the hustle of our everyday lives, we, too, can get confused when we try to keep too many things going at once. Yet whenever we are confused or make mistakes, we have the assurance that God is always there and we can call on Him, day or night, even for the simplest tasks. If we trust our own judgment, rather than seeking His, we will likely become confused and make poor choices. God has the answers to all our confusion. "God is not the author of confusion, but of peace, as in all churches of the saints" (1 Corinthians 14:33).

FOOD FOR THOUGHT

Let prayer be the key to the day,
and the bolt to the night.

FOOD FOR THE BODY

Sausage and Gravy
Ingredients:
  ¼ cup butter
  2 pounds sausage
  1¼ cups flour
  2 quarts milk
  Salt
  Pepper
  Seasoned salt

In a large skillet, melt the butter, then fry the sausage until browned. Add flour and stir well. Slowly stir in milk. Continue to stir until gravy thickens. Add more milk if too thick. Add the seasonings to taste.

LIZZIE MILLER

WHO BUT GOD?

I will not leave you comfortless: I will come to you.
JOHN 14:18

With a heavy heart, Esther left her son Noah's bed and headed for the mailbox. When Noah was fourteen, he'd been diagnosed with bone cancer, but the cancer had recently spread to Noah's lungs and had affected his breathing. The doctor said it was only a matter of time until Noah's life would end, and Esther wanted to spend as much time with her precious boy as possible.

Esther reached into the mailbox and withdrew a stack of letters. She was surprised to see that one of them was from her sister, Betty, who had offered in a previous letter to come stay with the family as Noah's time drew near. Since Esther didn't know when to tell Betty to come, she hadn't yet responded.

She tore open the letter and began to read.

Dear Esther:

I wanted you to know that I'll be arriving on Friday morning. Could you please have someone come to the bus station to pick me up?

Esther blinked against burning tears. *Does Betty know something we don't? Has God laid it on my sister's heart to come now?*

The following day, Esther was surprised when a knock sounded at the door and she discovered her closest neighbor, Sarah, standing on the front porch.

"I've brought you a casserole dish," Sarah said. "And I can stay to help with anything that needs to be done."

Overcome with appreciation, Esther could barely speak. "Danki, Sarah."

A short time later, Janet, an English neighbor, and Katherine, another Amish friend, came over. One by one, each family member showed up, and everyone gathered around Noah's bed. That evening, Noah passed peacefully from this life to the next.

Despite her sorrow, Esther felt joy in knowing that God had summoned her friends and family when they were needed the most. "Who but God knows exactly what we need, when we need it?" she whispered.

There are many times when we are unable to do anything about our external circumstances. Those are the times that we need to remember to call on God, for He is only a prayer away.

God feels our pain and is always there to offer comfort when we endure sorrows. He often uses friends and family to minister to us during difficult times. God will give us the strength and energy to make it through the hardest of times.

When someone else is going through difficult times, we should be sensitive to God's calling so that we may minister to those in need.

FOOD FOR THOUGHT

When we have nothing left but God,
we will find that He is enough.

FOOD FOR THE BODY

Cabbage Casserole
Ingredients:
　　½ cabbage, medium, finely chopped
　　Salt
　　½ cup rice, uncooked
　　½ cup chopped onion
　　1 pound ground beef
　　Salt
　　Pepper
　　1½ cups tomato juice

Preheat oven to 350 degrees. Spread half of the cabbage in the bottom of a roasting pan. Sprinkle with salt. Add rice, onion, and meat. Spread remaining cabbage on top. Add salt and pepper to taste. Cover with tomato juice. Bake for 1½ hours or until done.

MRS. WILLIAM MILLER

THE GIFT OF LOVE

*If we love one another, God dwelleth in us,
and his love is perfected in us.*

1 JOHN 4:12

Are you coming to bed, or did you plan to stay up all night working on your quilt?"

Mavis leaned away from the quilting rack and glanced at her tall, bearded husband. "Why don't you go ahead, James? I have a little more I want to do, and then I'll be up."

He shook his head. "Why are you pushing yourself so hard to get that done? It's not like your sister's birthday is tomorrow, you know."

Mavis held up one corner of the blue and white Dahlia pattern she'd begun piecing together some time ago. She had planned to present the quilt to Sadie for her birthday, but Sadie had recently become ill and was in the hospital recovering from an emergency appendectomy.

"I don't want to wait until my sister's birthday," she told her husband. "If I give the quilt to Sadie now, it might cheer her while she's recovering."

James kissed the back of Mavis's neck. "You're a fine example of the way we should show love to others."

Mavis stood and gave James a hug. "Sometimes, when we get busy with our own lives, we forget to offer sacrificial love to others. I'm glad for the reminders we have in the Bible."

He nodded. "Jah, me, too."

We can show others we love them in many ways—through a sacrificial gift, a kind word, or a friendly smile. God loves us so much that He sent His Son to die for our sins. Shouldn't we find ways to show our love to others?

"And now these three remain: faith, hope and love. But the greatest of these is love" (1 Corinthians 13:13 NIV).

FOOD FOR THOUGHT

Life without love is like a day without light.

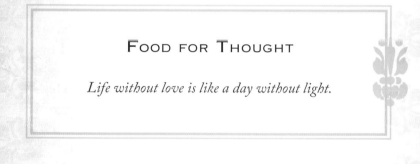

Cinnamon Raisin Bread
Ingredients:
  1 cup milk, scalded
  ¼ cup butter
  1 tablespoon yeast
  1 teaspoon sugar
  2 tablespoons warm water
  1 egg, slightly beaten
  ½ cup raisins, boiled
  4 cups bread flour
  ¼ cup sugar
  Cinnamon

In a kettle, heat milk and butter until lukewarm. Dissolve yeast and 1 teaspoon sugar in warm water. Stir yeast into milk mixture. Add egg and raisins. Mix with bread flour and remaining sugar until thoroughly blended. Let rise, then roll dough into an even layer ½ inch thick. Sprinkle with cinnamon. Roll up and put in 3 bread pans. Let rise. Preheat oven to 350 degrees. Bake for 40–45 minutes.

MRS. JACOB STUTZMAN

CLOSE CALL

For the eyes of the Lord are over the righteous,
and his ears are open unto their prayers.

1 PETER 3:12

I'm eager to get to the farmer's market," Donna told her husband as they headed down the road toward the town of Bird in Hand on Saturday morning. "I hope they have lots of pickled red beets today, because those are my favorite."

Ken glanced over at her and smiled. "I think you like all the Pennsylvania Dutch foods that are available at the market."

She nodded. "I guess that's true."

As their station wagon approached the next intersection, the car in front of them slammed on its brakes. Ken did the same, and they screeched to a stop just in time to keep from hitting the other vehicle.

"That was a close call," Donna exclaimed.

Ken looked in his rearview mirror, and his eyes became huge. "I'll say! The horse and buggy following behind nearly rear-ended us."

Donna turned around, amazed at the sight that greeted her. The neck of a dark brown horse was pressed up against their back window.

Ken put the station wagon in PARK and got out. Donna did the same. When they rushed around back, they discovered the horse's head resting on the roof of their vehicle, which was why they had been able to see his neck in the rear window.

"Are you folks all right?" Ken asked the driver of the buggy, a young Amish man, who was with a wife and three small children.

"Jah, we're fine, but that was a close call," he said, backing his horse and buggy slowly away from the station wagon. "God must have been watching out for us."

Donna nodded as tears clouded her vision, and she said a quick prayer of thanks for all of them.

Sometimes when we are involved in a scary situation, we can see clearly how God has protected us. There are probably a lot more times that we'll never realize God has kept us from harm. Even so, we should thank Him daily for His love and protection.

"For he shall give his angels charge over thee, to keep thee in all thy ways" (Psalm 91:11).

FOOD FOR THOUGHT

God does not shield us from life's storms;
He shelters us in life's storms.

FOOD FOR THE BODY

Pickled Red Beets
Ingredients:
> Fresh beets
> 4 cups water
> 2 cups cider vinegar
> 7 cups sugar
> 3 teaspoons salt

Cook whole beets in water until tender. Remove the beets. Set water aside. Cool beets under running water, then peel. Beets can be sliced or left whole. Mix water from beets with vinegar, sugar, and salt. Add the cooked beets to this mixture, then heat in an open kettle for approximately 15 minutes. Put into sterilized canning jars and seal.

CLARA MAST

NO PEEKING

Take therefore no thought for the morrow:
for the morrow shall take thought for the things of itself.
MATTHEW 6:34

Let's play hide-and-seek," young Clara suggested to her brother, Andrew. "And no peeking this time."

Katherine, their mother, chuckled and reached into the wicker basket at her feet. She plucked out a pair of her husband's trousers and hung them on the clothesline. She had always enjoyed seeing her children play together.

Katherine shielded her eyes from the morning sun as she watched Clara run to the barn. Andrew covered his eyes, so he wouldn't peek, and it made her think of the No-Peek Stew she had placed in the oven early this morning. It would be ready for their noontime meal, and she planned to make a pan of biscuits and a tossed green salad to go with it.

"Ready or not, here I come!" Andrew swished past his mother, causing her long green dress to blow in the breeze.

Katherine smiled as her son ran through the yard, looking under the porch and behind every bush. She knew he wanted to know where his sister was hiding, and no doubt, he had been tempted to peek.

So many times I've wished that I could see into the future, she mused. *But I know my focus should be on today.* She reached for another pair of Abe's well-worn trousers and smiled. *There's no point in trying to peek into the future.*

In Matthew 6:33, Jesus said, "But seek ye first the kingdom of God, and his righteousness; and all these things shall be added unto you."

God wants us to leave the future in His hands, knowing He will be there to help us through anything that might occur. If we become concerned about the things that might happen, we will lose sight of the joy God has given us today. It's never good to try to peek into the future or worry about what lies ahead. Our future is in God's hands, and He will see us through.

FOOD FOR THOUGHT

You can't see around the corners, but God can.

No-Peek Stew
Ingredients:
- 2½ pounds stewing beef, cut fine
- 1 onion, chopped
- 6 carrots, diced or cut
- 2 potatoes, cubed
- 1 teaspoon sugar
- 1 stalk celery, thickly sliced
- 2 cups tomato juice
- 2 teaspoons salt
- 2½ teaspoons Minute Tapioca

Preheat oven to 250 degrees. Place all ingredients in an oven-safe casserole dish. Cover tightly. Bake for 4 hours. No need to peek at this delicious stew.

Mrs. Jacob Stutzman

A Stranger's Trust

*The LORD is good, a strong hold in the day of trouble;
and he knoweth them that trust in him.*

NAHUM 1:7

That store run by the Amish family sure had some interesting things for sale, didn't it?" Janet said to her husband, Bret, as they climbed into the car.

He buckled his seat belt and smiled. "For you, I guess. Just lots of straw hats and plain white hankies on the shelves for the men."

Janet was about to comment when she heard a siren blaring in the distance. "Sounds like there might be a fire somewhere," Bret said.

Just then, the Amish man who ran the store they'd just left ran out the door, grabbed a scooter that had been parked near the side of the building, and started down the driveway. He stopped when he reached their car and knocked on Bret's window.

"Can I help you?" Bret asked after he'd rolled down the window.

"I was wonderin' if you would mind givin' me a ride to the fire station," the Amish man said. "I'm part of the volunteer fire department, and I could get there much quicker in your car than I can on my scooter."

Bret glanced over at Janet, and she shrugged, then nodded.

"Sure. Hop in the backseat," her husband said.

Without a moment's hesitation, the Amish man dropped

his scooter in the grass, opened the back door, and climbed in. "The station's up the street about a mile on the right," he said.

As they continued up the road, Janet noticed several Amish men riding scooters. *Are they all headed to the firehouse?* she wondered.

When they pulled into the driveway of the station, Janet had her answer. Amish men on scooters, and some who had received rides in cars, poured into the fire station, donned their fireman's hats and coats, and climbed aboard the fire trucks that were preparing to answer a call.

The Amish storeowner offered his thanks, exited the car, and sprinted toward the firehouse to join the others.

"Can you believe that?" Janet said with a shake of her head.

Bret looked over at her. "What?"

"That Amish man was so trusting. He'd never met us before. We are complete strangers, and yet he trusted us enough to get into our car and take him where he needed to go."

Bret smiled and nodded. "I guess not everyone in the world is suspicious of strangers." He paused, looking at the men clambering over the fire equipment. "Especially if they trust in God first."

Although we can't trust everyone we meet, there is One we can always trust. When you allow God to control your life and put your trust in Him, He will give you internal and eternal peace. After all, God is all-knowing, all-loving, all-powerful, all-forgiving, and He will show you His plan for your life if you trust Him.

"It is better to trust in the LORD than to put confidence in man" (Psalm 118:8).

FOOD FOR THOUGHT

Faith is not belief without proof
but trust without reservation.

Chocolate Mocha Pie

Ingredients:

> 1 tablespoon gelatin
> ¼ cup cold water
> 2 tablespoons cocoa
> 1 teaspoon instant coffee
> 1¼ cups milk
> ¾ cup sugar
> ⅛ teaspoon salt
> 1 cup whipping cream
> 1 teaspoon vanilla
> Chopped nuts
> Pie shell, baked

Soak the gelatin in the cold water. Set aside. Combine the cocoa, coffee, milk, sugar, and salt in a saucepan, and bring to a boil, stirring constantly. Remove from heat. Add the gelatin mixture, cool until slightly thickened. Beat the cooked mixture until smooth. Remove from heat and cool. In a separate bowl, beat the whipping cream and vanilla. Fold the whipped cream into the cooled pie mixture. Pour into a baked pie shell and top with nuts.

Lizzie Miller

SONG OF PRAISE

I will praise thee, O LORD, with my whole heart;
I will shew forth all thy marvellous works.
PSALM 9:1

I have a favor to ask," Anna's sister, Mary, said as she entered the house carrying a yellow canary in a small cage.

"Are you making a trip and want me to care for Sunshine while you're gone?" Anna asked.

Mary placed Sunshine's cage on one end of the kitchen counter. Then she removed her dark bonnet and black shawl, hanging them on a wall peg near the door. "I'm not going anywhere right now, but I was hoping you could keep my canary for a while."

Anna tipped her head. "How come?"

"Sunshine won't sing anymore, and I thought maybe some time spent with your canary would get her warbling again."

Anna nodded. "That might work. We'll put their cages next to each other for a few days and see what happens."

For the next week, Anna listened for any musical sounds coming from her sister's bird, but Sunshine remained quiet. It was a puzzle, and even though Anna knew it might seem like a small thing to ask, she prayed that if God wanted the canary to sing again, He would tell her what to do.

One day, while Anna was making supper, an idea popped into her head. Maybe the bird needed a new cuddle bone. She examined the old one in Sunshine's cage and discovered that it had worn down, which meant the canary's beak wasn't being properly sharpened.

She replaced Sunshine's cuddle bone, and soon he began to sing. Anna's bird, Petunia, trilled along with Sunshine, making the kitchen the most joyous room in the house.

Anna smiled. The canaries' songs had made her feel happy, too, and she praised God for answering her prayer and for creating such beautiful creatures and their joyous songs.

God has given us many wonderful things to praise Him for—answered prayer, our daily provisions, good health, family, friends, and most of all, His Son, Jesus. The next time you hear a bird sing, why not use it as a reminder to lift your voice in praise to God?

"Rejoice in the LORD, O ye righteous: for praise is comely for the upright" (Psalm 33:1). God truly is worthy of our praise!

FOOD FOR THOUGHT

When you sing your own praises, you always get the tune too high; when you sing God's praises, you can never go high enough.

Plate Salad

Ingredients for salad:

    ¼ head cabbage, shredded

    ½ head lettuce, shredded

    3 hard-boiled eggs, shredded

    2 carrots, grated fine

    6 stalks celery, cut fine

    2 green peppers, cut fine

    1 large tomato, cut fine

    Cheese, shredded

    Cracker crumbs

Ingredients for dressing:

    1 cup mayonnaise or Miracle Whip

    1¼ teaspoons salt

    1 tablespoon mustard

    ¾ cup sugar

    A dab of milk

Layer the first 7 salad ingredients on a large plate. Mix the dressing ingredients and spoon over salad. Add a layer of shredded cheese and cracker crumbs.

MRS. WILLIAM MILLER

WISE ANSWERS

If any of you lack wisdom, let him ask of God,
that giveth to all men liberally, and upbraideth not;
and it shall be given him.

JAMES 1:5

As Lettie set out the ingredients for that evening's supper, she thought about the discovery her husband, Luke, had recently made in the pasture. One of his mares had delivered a stillborn colt. Another mare had died while giving birth to its baby. Now Luke had one mare and one colt that needed each other, but the mare knew the baby wasn't hers, and she would not accept it.

Lettie closed her eyes in prayer. "Luke needs wisdom in knowing what to do. Will You show him, Lord?"

An hour later, Luke finally came into the house. He removed his straw hat and placed it on the stool near the door, then rushed over to Lettie. "The mare has accepted the orphaned baby!" he said excitedly. "The colt is having her first taste of mother's milk, and I'm thankful that God gave me the wisdom to know what to do."

Lettie gave her husband a hug. "What did you do, Luke?"

"I rubbed some of the placenta from the dead foal on the baby that lived." He grinned. "When I lost one colt and one mare, I was afraid I might lose the other colt as well, but God helped me figure out what to do."

How many times have we been faced with a problem for which there seemed to be no answers? If we trust in our own wisdom, we might make a mistake, but if we turn to God for guidance, He will help us make a wise decision.

In Proverbs 2:6, we are reminded: "For the LORD giveth wisdom: out of his mouth cometh knowledge and understanding." May we always remember to seek God's will in all that we do.

FOOD FOR THOUGHT

If you can't have the best of everything,
make the best of every thing you have.

FOOD FOR THE BODY

Woodchopper's Hash
Ingredients:
    2 tablespoons shortening
    5 potatoes, medium, peeled and diced
    1 quart green beans, drained
    ½ cup chopped onion
    3 slices bread, cubed
    4 eggs, beaten

Melt the shortening in a large skillet. Fry the potatoes until soft, add the beans, then the onions and bread. Fry until tender, then add eggs, without stirring. Cook a few minutes, until the eggs are set, then turn to brown.

MRS WILLIAM MILLER

NOTHING'S IMPOSSIBLE

For which cause we faint not;
but though our outward man perish,
yet the inward man is renewed day by day.
2 CORINTHIANS 4:16

A terrible racket woke Fern early one Saturday morning, and she scrambled out of bed. "I wonder what's going on outside," she said to her husband, Willard, who was also awake.

"Guess we'd better find out." Willard rushed to the window, and Fern did the same. She lifted the dark shade and gasped. Pounding hailstones poured from the sky, covering the deck and beating the plants in their yard to shreds.

"Such weather we're having for this time of the year," Willard mumbled with a shake of his head.

Fern nodded. "I've never seen this much hail come down in the month of September before. My beautiful flowers will all be gone."

When the hail stopped coming down and the couple had gotten dressed, they headed outside to survey the damage.

"See that pile of hailstones?" Willard pointed to a spot near the front step. "I'll bet it's nearly a foot deep!"

"The tender leaves on the trees look pathetic. It's impossible for anything to have survived that storm," Fern said as she glanced around a yard that had been bursting with color yesterday. She started to head back inside, but Willard stopped her.

"Look there, at that patch of hail near the maple tree." He pointed across the yard.

Fern's face broke into a smile. "Oh, Willard, there's a purple pansy sticking its head out. I guess everything didn't die after all."

He reached over and took hold of her hand. "Even if the flowers and leaves hadn't made it, most likely they would have come back next spring."

There are many times when we feel weighed down by unexpected, unpleasant circumstances. But with God nothing is impossible. He gives us promises like the one found in Lamentations 3:22–23: "It is of the LORD's mercies that we are not consumed, because his compassions fail not. They are new every morning: great is thy faithfulness."

Even when the burdens of life take us down, through Christ we can be renewed in spirit every day.

FOOD FOR THOUGHT

God does not spare us trials,
but He helps us overcome them.

FOOD FOR THE BODY

Impossible Cheeseburger Pie
Ingredients:
   1 pound ground beef or sausage
   ½ cup chopped onion
   ½ teaspoon salt
   ¼ teaspoon pepper
   1½ cups milk
   3 eggs
   ¾ cup Bisquick
   ½ pint pizza sauce
   1 cup shredded cheese

Preheat oven to 400 degrees. In a large skillet, brown the meat and onions. Add salt and pepper, then spread in a 9-inch pie pan. Set aside. Beat milk, eggs, and Bisquick together until smooth. Pour over the meat and bake for 30 minutes or until knife comes out clean. Top with pizza sauce and cheese.

CLARA MAST

A SPECIAL GIFT

And my people shall be satisfied
with my goodness, saith the LORD.
JEREMIAH 31:14

Phoebe sank wearily to the sofa, feeling as though the weight of the world rested on her shoulders this morning. She placed her hands against her protruding stomach. *I believe it's the weight of this baby, as well as my many chores, that is getting me down.*

Phoebe and Harold already had eight children, and she wondered if she could manage another one. There was always so much to do—clothes to be washed, a house needing to be cleaned, cooking, ironing, and gardening. On days like today, Phoebe didn't know if she could take another step, much less make the special treat she had promised her children.

Alma, who had recently turned five, sashayed up to her mother and said, "Mama, are ya ready to put the peanut butter patties together?"

Phoebe wiped the perspiration from her forehead. "Can you wait awhile? Your *mamm's* [mom's] feeling kind of tired right now."

"That's all right, I'll do it," Sharon, who was ten years old, offered. "Peanut butter patties aren't so hard to make."

Phoebe smiled gratefully. "Danki, Sharon. I appreciate the help."

When Sharon hurried off to the kitchen, Phoebe thought Alma would do the same. Instead, the child took a seat on the sofa and placed one hand on her mother's stomach. "When the *boppli* [baby] comes, can we keep it?" she asked, lifting her innocent gaze toward Phoebe. "I'm really wantin' a little *bruder* [brother] or *schweschder* [sister], and I promise to help as much as I can."

Phoebe nodded as tears clouded her vision. "Of course we'll keep the boppli. Every one of my children is God's special gift." She leaned over and kissed the top of her little girl's head. "Right now, I'm counting my blessings."

Like Phoebe, we may sometimes feel overwhelmed because of so many responsibilities. Some may have a houseful of children or feel exhausted due to all the chores needing to be done. Others might feel stressed with the demands of a job outside the home, or from commitments made to church or other organizations.

Taking time to think about the blessings God has given us can help redirect our thoughts and help us prioritize. Children are one of God's special gifts, and so is each new day He gives us.

The next time you feel stressed, a good antidote is to take time out to reflect on everything God has given to you.

FOOD FOR THOUGHT

When I come to the end of my rope,
God is there to take over.

FOOD FOR THE BODY

Peanut Butter Patties
Ingredients:
> 2 pounds powdered sugar
> 6 cups crispy rice cereal
> 4 cups crunchy peanut butter
> 1 cup margarine
> ¼ teaspoon salt
> Sweetened chocolate squares, melted

In a large bowl, mix the sugar, cereal, peanut butter, margarine, and salt until thoroughly blended. Form into small patties. Dip into the melted chocolate and serve.

ESTHER RABER

WELL HIDDEN

For in the time of trouble he shall hide me in his pavilion:
in the secret of his tabernacle shall he hide me;
he shall set me up upon a rock.
PSALM 27:5

Bernice had just hung the last towel on the clothesline when her daughter, Katie, came out of the barn carrying an orange and white striped cat.

"I see you found Callie," Bernice said as Katie came near. "I haven't seen her around for several days and figured she'd gone off somewhere to have her *busslin* [kittens]."

Katie nodded. "Papa found Callie and six babies wedged between the horse stall box and the outside wall, and it's such a tight fit that poor Callie has to lie on her back to nurse them."

"So what's your *daed* [dad] doing about it, and how come you're holding Callie?"

"Papa's fixed her a nice bed in the hay, and he's puttin' the busslin there right now." Katie stroked the cat's ears. "I brought Callie outside so she wouldn't get upset when Papa moved them."

"I hope it works." Bernice picked up her laundry basket. "I'll call you when it's time to set the table for lunch."

Some time later, as Bernice was slicing bread for sandwiches and Katie was setting the table, Bernice's husband came into the house, shaking his head.

"What's wrong, Abe?" Bernice asked with concern. "You look frustrated."

"That silly *katz* [cat] of ours won't stay in the nest of hay I made for her and the busslin." He shook his head. "As soon as I turned my back, she took her babies right back to that narrow place in the horse's stall."

"Maybe Callie thinks her little ones are better off there," Bernice said. "After the last batch of busslin got trampled by the horse, she's probably decided that the best way to protect her little family is to keep them well hidden."

Abe smiled and kissed his wife and daughter. "I guess she's just trying to take care of them, like we do with our little ones and God does with us."

Just as a mother cat cares for and protects her young, or as we do with our children, our loving heavenly Father watches out for us. We are His children, and when we are in danger, God hides us in the cleft of the rock, under His wing, and in the shadow of His hand.

"Thou art my hiding place; thou shalt preserve me from trouble; thou shalt compass me about with songs of deliverance" (Psalm 32:7).

FOOD FOR THOUGHT

When the world around you is crumbling,
God is the rock on which you can stand.

FOOD FOR THE BODY

Underground Ham Casserole
Ingredients for first layer:
> 4 tablespoons butter
> 1 tablespoon Worcestershire sauce
> ¼ cup chopped onion
> 4 cups cubed ham

Ingredients for second layer:
> 2 cups Velveeta cheese
> 2 cups cream of mushroom soup
> 1½ cups milk

Ingredients for third layer:

    4 quarts mashed potatoes
    1 pint sour cream
    Bacon

Preheat oven to 350 degrees. Melt butter in a large roasting pan.
Stir in Worcestershire sauce, onion, and ham. Stir together cheese,
soup, and milk and add to butter mix. Blend together potatoes and
sour cream and add to pan. Put strips of bacon on the top and bake
for 1–1½ hours.

MIRIAM MILLER

FOLLOW THE LEADER

Be ye therefore followers of God, as dear children.
EPHESIANS 5:1

Orlie, would you run outside and feed the chickens?" Nora asked her nine-year-old son as she moved over to the sink to peel some potatoes.

"Sure, Mama. I can do that." Orlie bounded out the door.

As Nora picked up the first potato and began to peel it, she glanced out the window and spotted Orlie entering the chicken yard. Suddenly, he was surrounded by chickens—fat red hens, strutting roosters, and yellow peepers just getting their feathers. Orlie clapped his hands a couple of times and began marching around the yard. The chickens followed right on his heels.

Nora chuckled. "What a comical sight."

Finally, after several more minutes of parading, Orlie headed for the coop, where the food was kept in large plastic buckets.

Nora knew the routine. Her son would fill a coffee can with cracked corn and bring it outside to feed the chickens. But apparently the chickens didn't remember the routine, for every one of them followed the boy into the coop.

A short time later, Orlie stepped into the yard again, with a throng of chickens behind him. None of them left his side until he sprinkled the food onto the ground. Then they all scattered, pecking, clucking, and devouring the corn like hungry gluttons.

Nora moved away from the sink and reached for a kettle from the bottom cupboard. She had just placed the potatoes on the stove to cook when she heard the back door open.

Orlie stepped into the kitchen, carrying a fat red hen in his arms. "Look, Mama," he said with a grin. "She followed me up to the house."

Nora smiled. "That's because you're a good leader. She knows who will take care of her."

Recognizing a good leader can be vital, and we know we can trust God to always take care of us. Isaiah 58:11 says: "And the LORD shall guide thee continually." During Jesus' time of ministry on earth, many people who needed to be fed followed Him. They not only needed to be fed, they wanted to see miracles. Because of those miracles, many people found Christ as their Savior.

Jesus wants us to seek His will and follow Him so that He can meet our physical and spiritual needs. May we always follow the right leader.

FOOD FOR THOUGHT

If we let God guide, He will provide.

FOOD FOR THE BODY

Lemon Cake
Ingredients:
1 box lemon cake mix
Butter
1 small box lime gelatin
¾ cup boiling water
¾ cup cold water
1½ cups milk
1 small box instant lemon pudding mix
½ cup Cool Whip

Bake the lemon cake, following the directions on the box, but adding a little extra butter to the batter. Set aside and cool. When cool, make holes all over the cake with a fork, about 1½ inches apart. Dissolve the gelatin in boiling water, then add the cold water. Pour over the cake and refrigerate. After cake has chilled, combine milk and instant pudding mix. Fold in Cool Whip and spread on the cake.

CLARA MAST

SWEET AS PUDDING

Children's children are the crown of old men;
and the glory of children are their fathers.
PROVERBS 17:6

Your mamm just gave you a little *bu* [boy]," Ruby announced to her nieces and nephews as she stepped out of her sister's bedroom and into the living room.

The children, ranging in age from three to eleven, stared at her with wide eyes and mouths hanging open.

"Can we see him?" nine-year-old Stephen asked, jumping up from the sofa.

"Soon," Ruby replied. "Your daed's with your mamm and the boppli now, but soon it will be your turn to go in and see him."

Ellie, who was seven, reached for her aunt's hand. "I think we should go down on our knees and thank God for givin' us a new little bruder."

Ruby nodded as tears welled up in her eyes. "That's a fine idea. Let's do it right now." She and the children knelt in front of the sofa and offered a silent prayer on behalf of their new little sibling.

Sometime later, the children were ushered into their parents' room. Everyone stood around their mother's bed, oohing and ahhing over the new baby.

"He's sweet as pudding," eleven-year-old Margaret murmured. "I can't wait to hold him."

The children's parents beamed with delight, and so did Ruby, for she had known that a new baby would be eagerly welcomed into this home.

Just as a baby is precious to his parents and siblings, so are we precious to our heavenly Father. In 2 Corinthians 6:18 we are reminded that God will be a father to us, and to our sons and daughters. In fact, the apostle Paul, in Romans 8:23, says God actually chooses to adopt us as His children.

Every child is precious in God's sight—including you!

FOOD FOR THOUGHT

Every child of God has a special place in His plan.

Date Pudding

Ingredients for syrup:
    1 cup brown sugar
    1 tablespoon butter

Ingredients for dough:
    ½ cup brown sugar
    ½ cup milk
    1 cup flour
    ½ cup chopped nuts
    2 teaspoons baking powder
    ¼ teaspoon salt
    1 cup dates
    Whipped cream

Preheat oven to 350 degrees. In a small saucepan, mix syrup ingredients and bring to a low boil. Pour into a greased 9 x 9-inch baking pan. Set aside. Mix ingredients for the dough and pour over the syrup mixture. Bake for 30 minutes. Cool and top with whipped cream.

MIRIAM MILLER

A TEMPTING THOUGHT

I have chosen the way of truth:
thy judgments have I laid before me.
PSALM 119:30

"Have you seen Nina?" Eunice asked her husband, Joel, when he entered the kitchen for an afternoon snack. "I've made haystacks, her favorite treat."

Joel shook his head and headed for the sink to wash his hands. When he was done, he said, "Your cousin Vera called over at my woodworking shop this morning and said she'd left her baby's diaper bag when she was here for church last Sunday. She was concerned because her wallet was in the diaper bag."

Eunice moved away from the cupboard and frowned. "I don't recall seeing it, do you?"

He shook his head as he sat at the table for a moment, munching a few of the haystacks. "I wonder if one of the other mothers might have taken it by mistake."

"I suppose that could have happened."

Just then, six-year-old Nina came into the kitchen, carrying her faceless doll. A few pieces of straw clung to the child's dark green dress, indicating that she had been playing in the barn. Her eyes lit up when she saw the haystacks sitting on the cupboard.

"You may have some as soon as you wash up," her mother said.

Nina pulled a stool over to the sink, and Joel looked over at Eunice and winked. "I'll be out in my shop if you need me."

When Joel left, Eunice took a seat at the table. "Vera forgot her baby's diaper bag when she was here on Sunday," she said after Nina had joined her. "Have you seen it?"

The child nodded, and her chin quivered. "I took it to the barn 'cause I thought I might need to change my dolly's *windel* [diaper]."

"Did you take anything from the bag?"

"Just the *windel*." Tears gathered in the corner of Nina's blue eyes. "I—I had a thought about takin' the wallet, but I knew it would be wrong."

Eunice pulled her daughter into her arms. "Thank you for being honest. I'm glad you didn't give in to your tempting thought."

We will always be faced with temptations, but with God's help we can resist temptation. Honesty is God's way, and He wants us to call on Him during times of temptation.

We are reminded in Proverbs 12:17, "He that speaketh truth sheweth forth righteousness; but a false witness deceit."

Food for Thought

Temptations are sure to ring your doorbell,
but it's your fault if you invite them for dinner.

Food for the Body

Haystacks

Ingredients:

    2 (18 ounce) packages butterscotch morsels
    ¾ cup peanut butter
    1 cup marshmallows
    1 cup chopped nuts
    1½ cups crispy rice cereal
    1 can chow mein noodles

In a double boiler, blend butterscotch morsels, peanut butter, and marshmallows until melted. Stir in the nuts, cereal, and noodles. Mix well and drop by spoonfuls onto wax paper. Cool and serve.

Mrs. Johnny Yoder

THROUGH THE EYES
OF A CHILD

God that made the world and all things therein,
seeing that he is Lord of heaven and earth,
dwelleth not in temples made with hands.
ACTS 17:24

Rebekah settled into the wicker chair on the back porch, with a pan of freshly picked green beans in her lap. It was a beautiful sunny day, with laundry flapping in the breeze, and birds chirping in the trees on the other side of the yard. Rebekah spotted her two oldest daughters, Rachel and Emma, who were weeding in the garden. So that Rebekah would be free to work on the beans, the girls had taken their three-year-old sister, Annie, with them, saying they would teach her how to pull weeds.

"Pull weeds, indeed." Rebekah smiled as she watched little Annie in her long blue dress parade up and down the garden rows in her bare feet, laughing and pointing to various things.

Suddenly, Annie halted, squatted in front of a huge cabbage plant, and squealed with delight. *"Gross kepp graut* [big head of cabbage]*!"*

Quickly, the little girl moved on, weaving in and out of the bean plants, until she came to row of green peppers.

Rebekah held her breath, waiting to see what Annie would do. She hoped Rachel and Emma were keeping an eye on their sister, because none of the peppers were ripe yet, and if Annie started picking them, they might not have enough when it came time for canning.

To Rebekah's surprise, Annie didn't pick a single pepper. She just stood there staring at them as though they were something special. Then she turned away and meandered into the tomato patch, stopping here and there to touch or smell some of the larger ones.

When Annie stepped out of the garden and onto the grass, Rebekah jumped to her feet. She was about to call out to one of the older girls to fetch their sister, when Annie flopped onto the grass. She leaned over, like she was studying it, reached out and gave it a couple of pats, then shouted, *"Graas* [grass]*! Es is nix driwwer* [there's nothing better].*"

Rebekah chuckled as she sat back down and started snapping beans. *Annie seems to realize that everything God made is wonderful and beautiful. Too bad we grown-ups don't take more time to enjoy the beauty He created just for us.*

Children see the world differently than most adults. They not only notice things but also will often take the time to study, touch, smell, and even taste the many astonishing things God has created for our enjoyment. Too often we adults become so busy with our daily chores and activities that we don't take the time to look for the small joys in life. We tend to be in too big of a hurry to notice the little things God created. If we're not careful, we can become numb to all the wonderful things around us.

We are reminded in Genesis 1:31: "And God saw every thing that he had made, and, behold, it was very good."

FOOD FOR THOUGHT

Don't overlook life's small joys while searching for the big ones.

Lemon Sponge Pie

Ingredients:

　　1 tablespoon butter

　　1 cup sugar

　　⅛ teaspoon salt

　　2 tablespoons flour

　　2 cups milk

　　2 eggs, separated

　　Juice and rind of 1 lemon

Preheat oven to 375 degrees. In a large bowl, blend together butter, sugar, salt, flour, and milk. In a separate bowl, beat the egg yolks. Stir the yolks, juice, and rind into the first mixture. Beat the egg whites until stiff and fold into the main bowl. Pour into an uncooked piecrust. Bake for 30 minutes or until solid.

MRS. ELI YODER

SENSE OF HUMOR

A merry heart doeth good like a medicine:
but a broken spirit drieth the bones.
PROVERBS 17:22

Would you see if there are any eggs in the henhouse?" Nancy asked her husband, Joshua. "I need more for the cake I'm making."

"Jah, sure. I'll be back soon." Joshua grabbed the basket Nancy had placed on the counter and headed out the door.

Nancy turned to her six-year-old daughter, Hannah, who was playing with her kitten in one corner of the room. "I'm going to check on the boppli. Let me know when Papa comes back with the eggs."

"Okay, Mama."

Nancy had just finished diapering the baby when she heard a yelp, followed by a loud *thunk*. She placed the baby in his crib and rushed into the kitchen. There sat her husband, sprawled on the floor with gooey, broken eggs all over his trousers.

Nancy covered her mouth with the palm of her hand. "What happened?"

Joshua narrowed his eyes and pointed at Hannah's kitten, which was cowering under the table.

"Sorry, Papa. I didn't mean for Mittens to get in your way," Hannah said with a catch in her voice.

Nancy watched her husband's serious expression blossom into a full-blown smile as he opened his arms to their daughter.

Hannah went willingly, and when Joshua encircled her with a hug, he began to chuckle. Soon the chuckle turned into a belly laugh, and tears streamed down his face. "I must look so *eefeldich* [silly], sitting here in the middle of the floor with messy eggs all over my clothes."

Nancy grinned back at him. She was glad her husband had been able to turn an unexpected accident into a humorous event. Getting upset wouldn't change what had happened, and grumbling wouldn't get the mess cleaned up any quicker. She was thankful to be married to a man with a merry heart.

It's not always easy to laugh at our distressing circumstances, but if we count our blessings and look for things to be joyous about, we will feel much better.

Only God can give the kind of joy that changes lives and reflects His love. That is why Psalm 144:15 tells us, "Happy is that people, that is in such a case: yea, happy is that people, whose God is the Lord."

Happy hearts make happy homes.

FOOD FOR THE BODY

Oatmeal Cake

Ingredients:

- ½ cup butter
- 1 cup boiling water
- 1 cup sugar
- 1 cup brown sugar
- 1½ cups flour
- 1 cup rolled oats
- 1 teaspoon baking soda
- Pinch of salt
- 2 eggs
- 1 teaspoon vanilla

Preheat oven to 350 degrees. In a large bowl, mix the butter, boiling water, and sugars together until the butter is melted. Add the flour, rolled oats, baking soda, salt, eggs, and vanilla. Mix well. Pour into a greased 9 x 13-inch baking pan and bake for 30–35 minutes.

MRS. JOHNNY YODER

GOING NOWHERE

Peace I leave with you, my peace I give unto you:
not as the world giveth, give I unto you.
Let not your heart be troubled, neither let it be afraid.

JOHN 14:27

Sylvia pulled out a chair and sat at the kitchen table so she could read the letter she had received from her cousin.

"What's Anita got to say?" Sylvia's elderly mother, Velma, asked. She sat in a rocking chair across the room, mending a hole in her husband's trousers.

"She says an outbreak of the chicken pox has kept many children in their community out of school this month." Sylvia clicked her tongue. "Sure hope the pox doesn't come our way. We've had enough sickness this winter."

"Worrying won't stop it," Velma said as she continued to rock. "If it comes, it comes."

"Anita also says they had another bad snowstorm." Sylvia looked up from the letter and shook her head. "I hope we don't get any more snow this winter. I worry about our roof caving in from the weight of it."

Velma kept right on sewing. "No need to worry about that, either."

Sylvia read on. "Anita's youngest girl has a croupy cough, and Ben, the oldest boy, got hit in the face with a snowball and lost a front tooth." She sighed. "Sure hope nothing like that happens to any of my *kinner* [children]."

Velma's chair stopped creaking. "I think you worry too much, Daughter."

Sylvia blinked. "I–I'm concerned."

"*Overly* concerned would be a better way to say it," her mother said with a shake of her head. "Worry is like rocking in a chair. It gives you something to do, but it never goes anywhere."

"You're right, Mom. I'll try to pray more and worry less."

Philippians 4:6–7 (NIV) offers a good alternative for worry: "Do not be anxious about anything, but in everything, by prayer and petition, with thanksgiving, present your requests to God. And the peace of God, which transcends all understanding, will guard your hearts and your minds in Christ Jesus."

Worry brings stress, and stress can cause illness. Prayer and faith bring the peace of God. Which would you rather have?

FOOD FOR THOUGHT

When worry knocks at the door, send faith to answer it—and you'll find no one is there.

Country Potato Pancakes
Ingredients:
  3 large potatoes, peeled
  2 eggs, slightly beaten
  1 tablespoon grated onion
  2 tablespoons all-purpose flour
  1 teaspoon salt
  ½ teaspoon baking powder
  Vegetable oil

Finely grate the potatoes into a bowl and drain any liquid. Add the eggs, onion, flour, salt, and baking powder. In a frying pan, add oil to the depth of ⅛ inch. Turn burner to medium and heat the oil. Drop potato batter by heaping tablespoons into hot oil. Flatten to form patties. Fry until golden brown, then turn and cook on the other side. Serve immediately. Makes about 24 potato pancakes.

Mrs. Jacob Stutzman

TOO BUSY FISHING

I press toward the mark for the prize
of the high calling of God in Christ Jesus.
PHILIPPIANS 3:14

I'm glad we could go fishing today," twelve-year-old Peter said to his cousin.

Ray nodded as he released his horse from the pony cart and tied him to a tree. "Jah, me, too."

Peter reached into the cart and grabbed his fishing pole and bait box. "Hope the fish are bitin' real good."

"Same here."

The boys settled on the grass near the water and cast out their lines. The sun felt warm, and insects buzzed overhead. Peter didn't mind; he'd been waiting all week to go fishing. Nothing could put a damper on his day.

Ray's horse let out a whinny, and Peter turned to see what was wrong.

"He's broken free—he's running away!" Ray hollered, scrambling to his feet.

"Aw, don't worry. He'll probably head for home."

Ray nodded and sat back down. "Guess I'll catch a couple of fish and then go after him."

A few hours and several fish later, Peter was surprised to see Ray's dad show up, leading the runaway horse. "When your pony came home without the cart or either of you, we began to worry," he said.

"He broke free from the tree where I'd tied him," Ray explained.

Uncle Willie reached under his straw hat and scratched his head. "And you didn't go after him?"

"We figured he'd gone home, so we decided to fish awhile and then go after him," Peter said.

Uncle Willie frowned. "I think you boys need to get your priorities straight. What would have happened if a car had hit the horse while he was out on the road? Was catching a few fish more important than the safety of your horse?"

Ray hung his head, and Peter did the same. "Sorry," they said in unison.

Peter looked at the fish lying beside his pole. His uncle was right; his priorities had been wrong.

Like Peter and Ray, mixing up our priorities can be pretty easy, especially when responsibilities conflict with our desires. When it comes to spiritual matters, however, making sure our priorities are straight is vital. It's good to ask ourselves once in a while if we are putting more emphasis on things that don't really matter than on things that count for eternity. As Luke 12:34 says, "For where your treasure is, there will your heart be also."

May we strive to remember to keep our priorities straight on the things that matter most.

FOOD FOR THOUGHT

*Success comes to the person who does today
what she's thinking of doing tomorrow.*

FOOD FOR THE BODY

Amish Cheese Dish
Ingredients:
    1 cup grated cheese
    2 eggs, beaten
    1 tablespoon butter
    1 cup bread crumbs
    1 cup milk
    Salt and pepper

Preheat oven to 350 degrees. Mix all ingredients together and pour
into a baking dish. Bake at 30 minutes or until nicely brown.

MRS. JACOB STUTZMAN

MISTAKEN IDENTITY

*For the L*ORD *seeth not as man seeth;*
for man looketh on the outward appearance,
*but the L*ORD *looketh on the heart.*
1 SAMUEL 16:7

I can't understand why this contrary horse won't let me hitch him to the buggy," Silas said to his wife as they prepared for a trip to town.

Irene climbed into the buggy. "Guess he wants to be stubborn this morning."

Silas struggled with the horse for several more minutes before he finally accomplished his task. "Sure hope he doesn't act up on the way to town." He took his seat on the driver's side, picked up the reins, and gave them a flick to get the horse moving.

Nothing happened. The horse didn't budge.

Silas tried again, this time offering a few words of encouragement to the stubborn animal. "Get up there, boy. Let's go now."

The horse whinnied and pawed at the ground.

Silas looked at Irene and frowned. "I may have to use the buggy whip, but I've never had to use it with this horse before."

Another horse and buggy came rolling into the yard just then. Silas's friend Levi was in the driver's seat.

"*Wie geht's* [how are you]?" Levi called.

"I'm doing fine," Silas replied. "Wish I could say the same for my horse."

"You mean *my* horse, don't you?"

Silas's forehead wrinkled. "Is your horse acting up, too?"

Levi pulled his buggy alongside of Silas's rig and climbed down. "The horse you've got hitched to your buggy is mine, and I've got yours."

Silas sat there several seconds, letting Levi's words sink in. "I wonder how that happened."

"We must have taken each other's horses when we left the Yoders' place after church yesterday." Levi stroked his own horse behind the ear. "They do look alike."

Silas chuckled. "No wonder I had such a hard time getting him hitched to the buggy. I should have realized he wasn't mine by the way he was acting."

"The poor horse wasn't really being stubborn," Irene put in. "It was just a case of mistaken identity."

As He did with Silas and Levi's horses, God makes each of us unique. While we might look similar to someone else, the way we act is proof of who we really are—and whose we are. It's important for Christians to do and say things that bring glory to God, so the world will know we belong to Him. If we live as God wants us to, there will never be cause for mistaken identity.

"For we are his workmanship, created in Christ Jesus unto good works, which God hath before ordained that we should walk in them" (Ephesians 2:10).

FOOD FOR THOUGHT

Others may be deaf to our words,
but they are never blind to our actions.

FOOD FOR THE BODY

Two-Hour Buns
Ingredients:
> 1½ packages yeast
> 1 cup warm water
> ¼ cup sugar
> 1 egg
> 2 tablespoons shortening
> ½ teaspoon salt
> 3½ cups bread flour

In a bowl, combine yeast, warm water, sugar, and egg. Beat until foamy. Add the shortening and salt. Mix well. Add the bread flour, mixing and kneading just until blended well. Let rise until double in size. Roll or shape into buns. Let rise again. Preheat oven to 400 degrees and bake for 15–20 minutes.

MRS. JACOB STUTZMAN

TRUE CHARACTER

The eyes of the LORD are upon the righteous,
and his ears are open unto their cry.
PSALM 34:15

A lump formed in Judith's throat as she entered her sister's hospital room. This morning Miriam had been involved in a buggy accident on her way to town. She'd suffered a mild concussion and had several broken bones. Just the week before, her husband had been kicked in the knee while he was giving one of their horses a shot, and he would be on crutches for a while. Their son had been hit in the forehead with a baseball a few weeks before that.

Judith took a seat beside Miriam's bed and struggled to keep her tears from spilling over. "What your family has been through these past few weeks doesn't seem fair," she said, gently touching Miriam's shoulder. "Are you feeling discouraged?"

Miriam shook her head. "When pain and suffering come, it's easy to feel sorry for ourselves. But that's when we should remember that God will give us strength to handle what life throws at us." Tears pooled in her eyes. "I'm thankful none of our injuries were life threatening, for they could have been much worse."

Judith nodded. "God was watching out for you."

"Our friends and family have been there for us, bringing in meals, cleaning the house, and helping wherever it's needed," Miriam said. "When it's our turn to help others, we'll remind them that God will see them through."

Throughout our lives there will be times when suffering and

unpleasant things come our way. But God promises He will never leave us or forsake us. He is always there to see us through the hard times.

A verse of scripture to help during difficult times is Psalm 34:17: "The righteous cry, and the Lord heareth, and delivereth them out of all their troubles."

The trials we encounter reveal our true character. When others are faced with trials, we can ease their burden by helping whenever it's needed.

FOOD FOR THOUGHT

No matter how many trials come our way,
God is only a prayer away.

Salmagundi

Ingredients for dough:

>   2 cups pastry flour
>   ½ teaspoon salt
>   ½ teaspoon baking powder
>   ⅔ cup shortening
>   ⅓ cup milk

Mix the dry ingredients thoroughly, then add shortening, chopping mixture into crumbs. Add milk and blend well. Roll out half of the dough and line a large pie pan with it.

Ingredients for filling:

>   4 cups finely diced potatoes
>   ½ onion, chopped
>   3 carrots, diced
>   ½ pound ground beef, browned
>   1½ cups pizza sauce
>   Grated cheese

Preheat oven to 350 degrees. Mix the filling ingredients and pour over dough in pie pan. Top with cheese. Roll out remaining dough and put on top. Poke holes in the top part of the dough with a knife and seal around the edges. Bake for 1 hour.

Mrs. William Miller

A STRONG BOND

Even a child is known by his doings, whether
his work be pure, and whether it be right.
PROVERBS 20:11

Rosanna slipped out of bed and followed her husband down the hall. It was three in the morning, and the temperature had dropped considerably, despite the fact that it was late spring. Rosanna knew the six hundred tomato plants they had set out the previous day were in danger of freezing.

"We'd better build a fire near the tomato patch," Owen said as they stepped into the kitchen. "Grab all the old newspapers you can find."

Rosanna scurried about the house in search of the newspapers, and Owen went out the door. A short time later he had a fire going, and the two of them fanned the flames to keep a cloud of smoke hovering over the tomato plants.

"We're almost out of newspaper," Owen said. "Is there more in the house?"

Rosanna shook her head, but before she could comment, their five children appeared, dressed in their nightclothes, carrying armloads of magazines.

"What are you doing out here in the cold?" she asked their oldest daughter.

"We heard you and Papa get up, and when we looked out the window and saw what you were doing, we decided to help," Karen replied.

Titus held up one of the magazines. "You can burn these, Papa. They're old, and we're done reading them."

Owen thumped his son on the back, and Rosanna's eyes welled up with tears. What a joy it was to know their children had come up with a plan to help save the tomatoes.

Several hours later the family stood together on the edge of the garden, marveling that a good frost had settled everywhere but on the tomato plants. Because of their strong family bond, they would have a fine tomato crop that could be sold at the market come summer.

Family life is the foundation of our society. There's something so special about the family unit that it makes those in our family become a part of our dearest earthly relationships. When family members pray together and work together, a lot can be accomplished and relationships become stronger.

An example for us to follow is found in the last part of Joshua 24:15: "But as for me and my house, we will serve the LORD."

How are things with you and your family today?

FOOD FOR THOUGHT

*No person can do everything,
but each one can do something.*

Baked Caramel Apples
Ingredients:
> Apples
> 2 heaping tablespoons clear gelatin
> 1¾ cups brown sugar
> Pinch of salt
> 3 cups water
> Chunk of butter
> 1 teaspoon vanilla
> Whipped cream

Preheat oven to 350 degrees. Peel enough apples to fill a baking pan. Cut in half, core, and line the pan with the apple halves. In a saucepan, combine gelatin, brown sugar, salt, and water. Cook until thick, stirring constantly. Add butter and vanilla. Pour over apples. Bake until apples are soft. Serve with whipped cream on top.

LIZZIE MILLER

TOO CLOSE FOR COMFORT

And be ye kind one to another, tenderhearted, forgiving one another,
even as God for Christ's sake hath forgiven you.
EPHESIANS 4:32

I would rather be doing anything but this, Selma thought as she stood near the septic tank opening, holding a lantern so her husband could see how full their tank had become.

"Can't you hold the light still?" Annoyance edged Jerold's voice, which only fueled Selma's irritation. "Would you bring it closer so I can see?"

"I'm doing the best I can," Selma snapped. "Maybe you'd rather do this alone?"

Before Jerold could reply, a flame shot up the hole, exploding near him and scorching his beard.

Selma jumped back as she dropped the lantern to the ground. "*Ach*, Jerold! Are you all right?"

He nodded. "That fire put a singe on my beard, and it sure taught me a good lesson."

"It's me who's to blame," she said tearfully. "I brought the lantern too close to the hole."

Jerold shook his head. "You only did what I asked." He reached for her hand. "Whew! I'm fortunate to have escaped this mishap with only a charred beard. It could have been much worse."

"I'm thankful you weren't seriously hurt, and I'm sorry for my unkind words and negative attitude."

"I'm sorry, too. Life is too short to let things come between us."

Selma nodded. "That fire shooting up the hole was too close for comfort."

It's human nature to feel irritation when we are faced with jobs we would rather not do, but it's never right to take our frustrations out on others. Proverbs 15:1 tells us: "A soft answer turneth away wrath: but grievous words stir up anger." How many arguments could be avoided if we learned to respond to others with a soft answer?

It shouldn't take a close call to help us remember to seek forgiveness when we have wronged another. It's always better to deal with problems in a loving way.

FOOD FOR THOUGHT

You can't speak a kind word too soon.

FOOD FOR THE BODY

Zesty Amish Meat Loaf

Ingredients for meat loaf:
- 1½ pounds ground beef
- ¾ cup rolled oats
- 2 eggs
- ¼ teaspoon pepper
- 2 teaspoons salt
- 1 cup tomato juice
- ¼ cup chopped onion

Ingredients for sauce:
- ½ cup brown sugar
- 2 teaspoons yellow mustard
- Dash of vinegar

Preheat oven to 350 degrees. In a large bowl, mix the ingredients for the meat loaf. Shape into a loaf and put in a baking pan. Bake for 45 minutes. In another bowl, mix the sauce ingredients, then put on top of the meat when it's finished baking. Bake for another 15 minutes or until done.

MRS. JACOB STUTZMAN

GOING TO THE DOGS

If we confess our sins,
he is faithful and just to forgive us our sins,
and to cleanse us from all unrighteousness.

1 John 1:9

"I miss Rose," Rudy told his mother when he entered the kitchen the morning after his dog disappeared. "Do you think she'll ever come home?"

Knowing how distraught her boy had been since Rose had gone missing, Alva replied, "When she gets tired of running all over the countryside and realizes how good she has it here, I'm sure she'll be back."

Rudy hung his head. "Sure hope so. Yesterday, Papa and I looked everywhere for her, but nobody we talked to had seen her."

Alva knew this wasn't the first time the sheltie had run away from home, and it might not be the last. But Rose would be welcomed home no matter how long she was gone. "Run outside and tell your daed and older brothers that breakfast is ready," she said, nodding at her son.

Rudy shuffled out the door. A few minutes later, he returned with the rest of the family. The five older brothers and Alva's husband, William, washed up at the sink, and everyone took seats around the kitchen table.

After their silent prayer, William announced, "Let's eat ourselves full!"

Halfway through breakfast, a knock sounded at the back door. "I'll get it," said Alva's oldest son, Lee.

When Lee returned a few minutes later, he was smiling and holding onto the collar of a disheveled-looking dog with its tail hanging between its legs.

"Rose, I've missed you!" Rudy jumped out of his seat and dashed across the room. He dropped to his knees and wrapped his arms around the grubby dog's neck. At the moment, Rose looked nothing like the beautiful flower for which she'd been named, but she certainly looked happy to be home. The wayward dog obviously knew her transgression had been forgiven, as she swiped Rudy's ear with her tongue and wagged her limp tail.

William looked over at Alva and winked. "Such a forgiving spirit our boy has when it comes to his dog."

Just as God forgives us when we have strayed, it's good that we should forgive ourselves. There are times when it's easier to forgive others than it is to forgive ourselves. Carrying guilt around is like moving through life with a bag of rocks tied to our back.

God wants us to learn from our mistakes, and the best remedy for remorse is to seek His forgiveness, apologize to whomever we have wronged, then forgive ourselves and move on.

FOOD FOR THOUGHT

Forgive someone—maybe even yourself. It will set you free.

FOOD FOR THE BODY

Cheddar Party Potatoes
Ingredients for potato mixture:
  2 pounds frozen hash browns
  1 pint sour cream
  1 can cream of chicken soup
  ½ cup chopped onion
  2 cups grated cheddar cheese
  ½ cup melted butter

Ingredients for topping:
  2 cups crushed cornflakes
  3 tablespoons melted butter

Preheat oven to 350 degrees. Mix ingredients for potato mixture and blend well. Place in a 9 x 13-inch baking dish. Mix together topping ingredients and layer on top of potatoes. Bake uncovered for 45 minutes to 1 hour. Serve hot.

Lizzie Miller

MAKING DO

Not that I speak in respect of want:
for I have learned, in whatsoever state I am,
therewith to be content.

PHILIPPIANS 4:11

Look at that fox squirrel over there," Susanna said to her three children as they walked through the woods bordering the back of their home.

Eight-year-old Molly pointed to the furry creature and giggled. "He's holdin' an ear of corn in his mouth while tryin' to dig a hole so he can bury it."

"I saw a squirrel take a green tomato right out of our garden the other day," Jonah, who was ten, piped up.

"That silly critter is gonna be disappointed when he realizes he can't store a tomato like a nut," twelve-year-old Willis said with a shake of his head.

Susanna nodded. "The squirrels are trying to get by with other food sources this year, since there aren't many nuts to be found."

"How come there aren't many nuts?" Jonah asked.

"We had late frosts in the spring, so the nut trees in the area didn't produce well." Susanna motioned to the acorn tree growing nearby. "There are hardly any acorns on the branches at all."

Molly tugged on the corner of Susanna's dark apron. "The squirrels won't starve to death, will they, Mama?"

"Not if they find other sources of food."

"Jah, just like that *schmaert* [smart] little squirrel with the corncob in its mouth," Willis said.

"That's right," Susanna agreed. "We could take a lesson from the animals that are learning to be satisfied and make do."

Jonah looked up at his mother with questioning eyes. "What can we learn from them?"

"We should learn to be content and enjoy what we have, rather than longing for the things we can't have," she explained. "We can make do with what's available and be thankful for whatever God provides."

We have so many things to be thankful for, and sometimes searching for ways to make do can be fun. Rather than complaining or feeling sorry for ourselves, we can learn to rely on God and be content with whatever He provides.

"Better one handful with tranquility than two handfuls with toil and chasing after the wind" (Ecclesiastes 4:6 NIV).

*Find contentment in enjoying the present
season instead of dreaming about the next.*

FOOD FOR THE BODY

Cream Cheese Nut Pie
Ingredients for pie filling:
  8 ounces cream cheese
  ½ cup sugar
  1 egg, beaten
  ½ teaspoon salt
  1 teaspoon vanilla
  2 piecrusts, unbaked
  1¼ cups chopped pecans

Ingredients for topping:
  6 eggs, beaten
  2 cups light corn syrup
  ½ cup sugar

Preheat oven to 375 degrees. In a mixing bowl, blend together the
cream cheese, sugar, egg, salt, and vanilla. Pour and spread into

unbaked piecrusts. Sprinkle pecans over the cheese mixture. In another bowl, beat together the topping ingredients. Pour over the nuts. Bake for 45 minutes. Makes two pies.

LIZZIE MILLER

PLEASANT WORDS

Whoso keepeth his mouth and his tongue
keepeth his soul from troubles.

PROVERBS 21:23

Lydia set the newspaper aside and looked over at her husband, who sat beside her on the porch swing. "There's sure been some unusual incidents happening around here in the last few weeks," she said.

Nate gave his beard a sharp pull. "Jah. My friend Sam had an interesting thing happen to him the other day."

"What was that?"

"Sam had taken his boys to the horse sale last Saturday, and I guess he got a good chewing out from a man who said Sam had misrepresented a horse he had bought from him." Nate paused and shook his head. "The other man said the horse balks, shies away from cars, and is downright stubborn. He kept going on and on about how he'd been cheated and said Sam would have to make things right."

"What did Sam say to that?"

"When he was finally able to get in a word, he told the man that he hadn't sold a horse here. Then the man calmed down and said, 'Since you're wearing the same color shirt as the fellow who sold me the horse, I just assumed it was you. I'm sorry for jumping to conclusions and for my unkind words.' " Nate folded his arms and leaned against the porch railing. "Hearing that story made me think about how everyone should guard their tongue."

Lydia nodded. "We should never fly off the handle at anyone, because we might have the wrong person. Besides, it's wrong to lose our temper in such a way."

In Proverbs 15:18, we are told, "A wrathful man stirreth up strife: but he that is slow to anger appeaseth strife." It's not always easy to control our temper, but speaking unkindly leads to problems. If we are slow to get angry we can usually avoid conflict with others.

In Proverbs 16:24, we learn that "Pleasant words are as an honeycomb, sweet to the soul, and health to the bones."

May we always strive to speak kind words to everyone we meet.

FOOD FOR THOUGHT

Nothing is opened more times by mistake than the mouth.

Upside-Down Amish Pizza

Ingredients for meat filling:

    2 pounds ground beef

    ½ cup chopped onion

    Salt and pepper to taste

    2 cups pizza sauce

    Pepperoni slices (if desired)

    1 cup chopped green peppers

    1 cup chopped mushrooms

    16 ounces sour cream

    Shredded mozzarella cheese

Ingredients for topping:

    2 eggs

    1 cup milk

    1 tablespoon oil

    ½ teaspoon salt

    ½ teaspoon baking powder

    1 cup flour

Preheat oven to 350 degrees. Brown the meat and onion in a skillet. Add the salt, pepper, and pizza sauce. Pour into a 9 x 13-inch baking pan. Layer with pepperoni, green peppers, and mushrooms. Bake for 15 minutes. Remove from oven and cover with sour cream and cheese. Set aside. In a bowl, mix all topping ingredients together and put on top of pizza. Bake for 30 minutes or until done.

MRS. JACOB STUTZMAN

CLOSE AT HEART

A man that hath friends must shew himself friendly:
and there is a friend that sticketh closer than a brother.
PROVERBS 18:24

As Mable took a seat on her daughter's bed, she noticed tears in the child's eyes. "What's wrong, Peggy? Why are you crying?"

"Sally's moving away, and I'm gonna miss her."

Mable nodded, remembering how sad she had felt this morning when she'd helped Sally's mother pack some of their belongings for their move to Indiana. She and Lois had been good friends since they were little, and their two youngest girls had become friends in the same way.

"It's always hard to say good-bye to friends," Mable said, taking Peggy's hand. "Your friendship with Sally doesn't have to end because she's moving away. You can write letters, and Sally's family will come back for visits."

Peggy sniffed. "Sally and I had fun baking cookies together. We won't be able to do that with her living far away."

"You can bake with me or your sisters."

"I know." Peggy scrunched up her pillow as more tears trickled down her flushed cheeks. "Do you think Sally will make new friends and forget me?"

"If you keep in touch through letters, I'm sure she won't forget." Mable wiped away her little girl's tears.

Peggy's eyes brightened some, and she placed one hand against her chest. "Me and Sally will never be far apart as long as I keep her close to my *hatz* [heart]."

The subject of friendship is important enough to be mentioned several times in the Bible. To make friends and keep them we must learn to be a friend by showing ourselves friendly and being there when our friends have a need.

Wouldn't it be nice to know that when people think about us they will remember the good things we've done for them? Likewise, it's good for us to appreciate the friends who have meant so much to us.

FOOD FOR THOUGHT

There is no scale or chart on earth to measure what a true friend is worth.

FOOD FOR THE BODY

Whoopie Pies
Ingredients:
 1 box chocolate cake mix
 1 cup flour
 Frosting (any kind)

Preheat oven to 400 degrees. Follow the directions on the mix, then add the extra flour. Mix thoroughly. Drop spoonfuls of batter onto a greased cookie sheet. Bake for 10–12 minutes. When cookies have cooled, put frosting between two cookies and cover each in cellophane wrap.

ANNA KING

SUPPLICATION

The LORD hath heard my supplication;
the LORD will receive my prayer.
PSALM 6:9

When the back door opened and slammed shut, Virginia knew her two youngest children must be home from school.

"I can't believe it's raining again," Jolene said as she stepped into the kitchen dripping water all over the floor.

"Yeah," her brother, Jeremy, agreed. "We're soaking wet."

Virginia handed them towels. "Hang up your coats, dry off as best you can, and come over to the table. I'll fix you some hot chocolate with marshmallows."

"That sounds good," Jolene said with an eager expression.

A few minutes later, Virginia and her children were gathered around the table with steaming mugs of cocoa.

"I don't like this nasty weather we're havin'," Jeremy complained. "I'll be glad when the sun comes out again."

"We should be grateful for the rain we're getting," Virginia said. "This morning I got a letter from your aunt Mary in Missouri, and she said it's been hot and dry there. She's worried they won't have a good crop of corn this year because they didn't get enough rain during the growing season."

Jolene took a sip from her mug. "Uncle Aaron needs that corn to feed his animals during the winter, doesn't he, Mama?"

Virginia nodded. "He sells a good deal of it, too."

"Wish there was something we could do to help out," Jolene said.

"Too bad we can't share some of our rain with the folks in Missouri," Jeremy put in.

Virginia smiled. "The best thing we can do for my brother and others who are affected by the drought is to make supplication for them."

"Supplication? What's that?" Jeremy wiped his mouth with the back of his hand and gave his mother a questioning look.

Virginia handed him a napkin. "It means we should offer prayers on their behalf."

"Let's do that," the children said in unison.

Their mother smiled, then reached out to take their hands. "Let's do it right now."

In 1 Thessalonians 5:17, we are told to "Pray without ceasing."

Praying for others should be a part of our daily prayer life. There are times when we don't know specifically how to help someone in need. Even when we can't help in a physical sense, we can still pray. Is there someone you should be praying for today?

FOOD FOR THOUGHT

*The best form of exercise is to touch
the floor regularly with your knees.*

FOOD FOR THE BODY

Missouri Grapenuts
Ingredients:
- 5 pounds brown sugar, or a little less if preferred
- 8 pounds whole wheat flour (about 24 cups)
- 1¼ tablespoons salt
- 2½ quarts buttermilk or sour milk
- 2 tablespoons baking soda
- ¾ cup margarine, melted
- 1½ teaspoons maple flavoring
- 2 teaspoons vanilla

Preheat oven to 350 degrees. In a large bowl, mix brown sugar, flour, and salt until thoroughly blended. In a separate bowl, combine buttermilk and baking soda, then add to the dry ingredients and mix well. Stir in margarine, maple flavoring, and vanilla. The dough should be fairly thick. Bake in a large pan for 45 minutes. Set aside when done. In two days, crumble fine and toast. (Recipe may be cut in half.)

MRS. WILLIAM MILLER

UNEXPECTED GIFT

The desire of a man is his kindness.
PROVERBS 19:22

As Mattie's husband, Lloyd, pulled their horse and buggy into their yard, she noticed something she hadn't seen when they'd left for town this morning. A huge stack of firewood was piled next to their barn.

"I wonder where that came from?" Mattie said, turning to Lloyd.

He shrugged. "Maybe one of our neighbors had extra and decided to share."

Mattie's eyebrows drew together. "How would anyone know we're in need of wood? I've not said anything, have you?"

Lloyd shook his head. "Didn't see the need. I knew the Lord would provide."

"That could be a note I see attached to one of the pieces of wood."

Lloyd climbed down from the buggy, and Mattie did the same.

"It's a note all right." He held up the piece of paper that had been taped to a hunk of wood.

"What does it say?"

Lloyd read the note out loud.

To Harvey and Edna:

    This is our wedding present to you. Since no one was here, we dumped it off, figuring you would see it when you got home.

                        Besht winche *[best wishes]*,
                           Emanuel and Amanda

Mattie gasped. "The wood wasn't meant for us at all. It was supposed to go to our newlywed neighbors who live two miles south of us. It must have been delivered to our place by mistake."

"As much as we need the wood, we surely can't keep it," her husband said.

"You'd best go inside for our boys and get them to help you load the wood onto our wagon so you can take it over to Harvey and Edna's place."

Before Lloyd could comment, a horse and buggy trotted into the yard, and Harvey stepped down.

"We have something of yours," Lloyd said when the young man approached.

"I know." Harvey chuckled. "Emanuel got a little confused when he gave directions to the men at the pallet shop."

Lloyd nodded. "My boys and I will see that it's returned right away."

Harvey shook his head. "Edna and I have plenty of wood to get us through the winter. So let's call this an unexpected gift from us to you."

Tears blinded Mattie's vision as she marveled at how quickly their needs had been met.

In Philippians 4:19 we are reminded that God will supply all our needs according to His riches. It should never come as a surprise when God provides. He sometimes uses other people to bless us with monetary things, and when we thank them, we should also remember to thank God for His unexpected gifts.

God blesses through His provisions—the giver and the receiver alike.

FOOD FOR THOUGHT

People seldom get dizzy doing good turns

Cottage Cheese Salad
Ingredients:
  2 boxes of gelatin (any flavor)
  2 cups boiling water
  1 cup whipped cream
  1 cup miniature marshmallows
  1 can crushed pineapple
  1 pound cottage cheese

In a mixing bowl, dissolve gelatin in boiling water. Place in refrigerator until it starts to thicken, then fold in the whipped cream, marshmallows, pineapple, and cottage cheese. Chill and serve.

MRS. WILLIAM MILLER

TIME TO HARVEST

He which soweth sparingly shall reap also sparingly;
and he which soweth bountifully shall reap also bountifully.

2 CORINTHIANS 9:6

As Dorothy and her daughter, Mary, stepped into the golden field of wheat carrying a jug of cold water and a basket of cookies, Dorothy was overcome with a sense of awe. Her husband, Reuben, and several of their Amish neighbors had been harvesting today. Next week, Reuben and the men would help harvest another Amish man's fields, and this would continue until everyone's fields had been done.

Dorothy shielded her face from the sweltering sun as she watched the crew of men cut and then bundle the grain, using mule-driven binders. Next, it would be stacked by hand into long lines of symmetrical shocks. Later, when the threshing crew came, everyone in the family would join in to help, as they carried the bundles of wheat to the threshing machine. There, the grain and chaff would be separated. Finally, the grains of wheat would be bagged and loaded onto the wagons. It was a tiring job, but with everyone working together to bring in the harvest, it would be done in an orderly, timely manner.

"We've brought you something cold to drink," Dorothy called to Reuben as he walked toward them.

"Jah, and some of your favorite cookies, too," Mary added.

He smiled. "Sounds good. I think all the men need a break."

"You've been working hard to bring in the harvest, but your labors will pay off when we have money from the wheat to buy the things we need," Dorothy said.

Reuben nodded. "Harvesting takes work, but we reap what we sow—it's always worth the effort."

In Matthew 9:37–38, Jesus told His disciples, "The harvest truly is plenteous, but the labourers are few; pray ye therefore the Lord of the harvest, that he will send forth labourers into his harvest."

God wants us to reap the harvest by telling others about His Son through our words and deeds. Bringing in the harvest is much easier when we have the help of others, but even if we must do it alone, our efforts will be blessed.

FOOD FOR THOUGHT

Have your harvest tools ready, and God will find work for you.

FOOD FOR THE BODY

Soft Batch Cookies
Ingredients:
- ½ cup butter
- ½ cup sugar
- ½ cup brown sugar
- 2 cups flour
- 1 egg
- 1 teaspoon vanilla
- 1 teaspoon baking soda, mixed with 1 drop of water
- 8 ounces chocolate chips
- ¼ cup nuts (optional)

Preheat oven to 350 degrees. In a large bowl, mix all ingredients in the order given. Pour into a greased baking pan, and bake for 10 minutes or until done. Do not bake until brown or it will harden. Cool and cut into bars.

CLARA MAST

ONE RUNG MISSED

But he giveth more grace. Wherefore he saith,
God resisteth the proud, but giveth grace unto the humble.
JAMES 4:6

I bet I can make it down the ladder faster than you," twelve-year-old Gideon bragged to his cousin, Naomi, who had recently turned thirteen.

Naomi peered over the edge of the hayloft. "It's a long ways to the bottom, and if you fall, you could get hurt. I think you'd better go down the ladder nice and easy."

Gideon folded his arms and lifted his chin. "I ain't afraid. I've gone up and down this ladder hundreds of times and never been hurt."

"You shouldn't *bralle* [brag] on yourself," Naomi said with a shake of her head. "And you shouldn't race down the ladder just to get someone's attention."

Gideon hesitated a moment, then whirled around and scampered down the ladder. He'd only made it halfway when he missed one rung and lost his footing. Down he went, landing on the floor with a thud.

Descending the ladder as carefully as she could, Naomi rushed to his side. "Gideon, are you all right?"

The boy moaned and sat up. "I don't think anything's broke. Just had the wind knocked out of me is all."

"But you could have been seriously hurt."

He nodded soberly. "You're right, and I shouldn't have been bragging or trying to prove how fast I was, either."

Naomi held out her hand. "Come on. Let's go into the house and play a game of checkers."

"I'll bet I can beat—" Gideon stopped in midsentence and smiled. "It doesn't matter who wins or loses."

The word *boast* means to praise. If our praise is for ourselves, it can turn into conceit, pride, or vanity, setting a bad example to others. Likewise, when we try to do everything in our own strength, it's a type of boasting. It's much better to ask the Lord to guide us.

In Proverbs 27:2, we are reminded, "Let another man praise thee, and not thine own mouth; a stranger, and not thine own lips." If we must boast, then let's boast on God, who has redeemed us and strengthens us each day.

The man who has a right to boast does not have to.

FOOD FOR THE BODY

Carrot Loaf
Ingredients:
    2 tablespoons butter
    1 onion, minced and sauteed in butter
    3 cups cooked and mashed carrots
    2 eggs, beaten
    1 cup milk
    1½ cups bread crumbs
    1 cup minced celery
    1 teaspoon salt

Preheat oven to 350 degrees. Sauté onion in butter. In a large bowl, combine butter, onions, and carrots. In a separate bowl, mix eggs, milk, and bread crumbs. Stir into carrot mixture, then add celery and salt. Shape into a loaf and place in a greased loaf pan. Bake for 40 minutes or until done.

MATTIE STOLTZFUS

LIKE A GOOD NEIGHBOR

*God is not unjust; he will not forget your work and
the love you have shown him as you have helped
his people and continue to help them.*
HEBREWS 6:10 NIV

I can't understand what could be keeping Eunice," Grace said to
her neighbor, Rosa, who sat beside her at the quilting frame.

"You're right," Rosa agreed. "It's not like Eunice to be late to
one of our quilting bees."

"Maybe I should ask Freeman to go looking for her. He's out
in the barn doing chores, but I'm sure he wouldn't mind."

Rosa glanced at the battery-operated clock on the wall. "That
might be a good idea. Eunice is almost an hour late."

Grace excused herself, knowing that the other nine women
who had come to help with her Dahlia quilt would get along fine
in her absence. When Grace stepped into the barn, the sweet
smell of hay assaulted her senses. Her husband had obviously
been caring for the livestock, although she saw no sign of him.

She cupped her hands around her mouth. "Freeman, where
are you?"

"Back here by the horses' stalls!"

Grace found Freeman forking hay into one of their buggy horse's stalls. "What's up?" he asked. "I thought you were busy with the quilting bee."

She nodded. "I am, but Eunice was supposed to be here, and she's almost an hour late. I'm getting concerned."

Freeman set the pitchfork aside. "Maybe I should head up the road and see if she's okay."

Grace smiled. Freeman had always been a good neighbor, and she was pleased that he was willing to go. "She's probably gotten busy with something, but just the same, I'd feel better knowing."

"No problem." Freeman reached for his straw hat, which hung on a nail, and started for the door. Grace followed. They had just stepped outside when a car came up the driveway.

A few seconds later, Eunice climbed out of the backseat. "Sorry I'm late," she said with a wave. "I lost a buggy wheel on the way over, and Kathy, my neighbor, was kind enough to give me a ride."

"Do you need someone to see that the horse and buggy are taken back to your house?" Freeman asked.

Eunice shook her head. "I appreciate the offer, but Kathy's husband, Tom, is there now, fixing the broken wheel. Sure is nice to have such good neighbors."

In today's busy world, there are many people who don't even know their neighbors, much less realize when they have a need. Luke 10:27 tells us, "Thou shalt love the Lord thy God with all thy heart, and with all thy soul, and with all thy strength, and with all thy mind; and thy neighbour as thyself."

If we took the time to become better acquainted with our neighbors and were willing to help in times of need, how much better our world would become.

FOOD FOR THOUGHT

*When you help someone up a hill,
you're that much nearer the top yourself.*

Chicken Corn Soup
Ingredients:
    1 large chicken
    2½ quarts water
    4 cups corn
    1 package egg noodles
    ½ teaspoon salt
    Dash of pepper

In a large kettle, boil the chicken in the water. When cooked thoroughly, remove the chicken, reserving the broth. Remove the meat from the bone and cut it into small pieces. Strain the broth, then add corn, noodles, chicken, salt, and pepper to taste. Cook until the noodles are soft. The amount of noodles added can be adjusted according to the thickness desired. The amount of corn and water can also be adjusted.

MATTIE STOLTZFUS

TOGETHERNESS

And let us consider one another to provoke
unto love and good works:
Not forsaking the assembling of ourselves together,
as the manner of some is; but exhorting one another:
and so much the more, as ye see the day approaching.
HEBREWS 10:24–25

Mildred looked around the room. Many of her friends, neighbors, and relatives had gathered at her and Mark's home today for their biweekly church service. It had taken a good deal of work to get the house cleaned and set up, which included removing the partitions between the living room and dining room, as well as setting up benches that would seat the people.

For a fleeting moment, Mildred had found herself wishing she didn't have to prepare for church today. Even this morning, when she'd awakened to the bright sunlight streaming through her bedroom window, she had wished she and her husband could have gone for a walk in the woods or taken a buggy ride to the nearby pond. *After all,* she'd reasoned, *God is there, same as He is here.*

Mildred's mother-in-law, Fannie, reached over and took her hand, pulling Mildred out of her musings. "*Is gut* [it's good] to be in church with other believers today, jah?" she asked with a warm smile.

Mildred nodded and relaxed on the backless wooden bench she shared with several other women as she opened her hymnbook to the song the *Vorsinger* [song leader] had announced. The steady, singsong voices of her friends and neighbors offered a sense of belonging and peace.

When Deacon Joe read a passage of scripture from Hebrews 10 about "not forsaking the assembling of ourselves together," Mildred knew she was exactly where the Lord wanted her this morning.

Have there been times when you felt too tired to get dressed and go to church? Perhaps, like Mildred, thoughts of other things filled your mind.

In Matthew 18:20, we are reminded, "For where two or three are gathered together in my name, there am I in the midst of them." While it's true that we can feel close to God in many different settings, the gathering together with other believers gives us a common bond and dispels loneliness. Worshiping with our friends and family not only draws us closer to them, but also to God.

FOOD FOR THOUGHT

Christians are like chunks of coal:
Together they glow, apart they die out.

FOOD FOR THE BODY

Caramel Dumplings

Ingredients for syrup:
- 2 cups boiling water
- 2 tablespoons butter
- ⅛ teaspoon salt
- 1½ cups brown sugar

Ingredients for dough:
- 1¼ cups flour
- 1 teaspoon baking powder
- ⅓ cup milk
- ⅓ cup sugar
- ⅛ teaspoon vanilla
- 2 teaspoons butter
- ¼ teaspoon salt

Mix ingredients for the syrup in a large kettle and let it come to a slow boil. Mix ingredients for the dough until thoroughly blended. Drop by spoonfuls into the boiling syrup. Cook 20 minutes, covered. Keep the syrup boiling slowly, so it doesn't cook away. Do not remove lid while it's cooking. Serve warm with ice cream.

Mrs. Johnny Yoder

A QUIET PLACE

He maketh me to lie down in green pastures:
he leadeth me beside the still waters.
He restoreth my soul:
he leadeth me in the paths of righteousness
for his name's sake.
PSALM 23:2–3

Ruth had been scurrying around all morning, baking bread, making homemade pickles, and washing the beets she'd picked from her garden. The kitchen was stuffy and hot, and she felt the weight of exhaustion.

She had just finished cleaning the kitchen when she heard a horse and buggy pull into the yard. She glanced out the window and saw her sister, Marilyn, step down from her buggy.

Ruth opened the back door as Marilyn walked onto the porch. "What a surprise! I didn't expect to see you until Sunday," Ruth said, motioning her sister to come inside.

Marilyn smiled and entered the house. "I felt like taking some time off today, and I thought you might like to go with me to a quiet place."

Ruth tipped her head in question. "It's not *friede* [quiet] at your place?"

"Not the kind of quiet I need when I'm feeling tired or stressed. Besides, when I'm at home I see all the work that needs to be done." She reached for Ruth's hand. "How about you? Wouldn't you like to take a little breather?"

Ruth nibbled on her bottom lip. "I really should clean the rest of the house, and then I need to—"

"You'll make yourself *grank* [sick] if you work too much," Marilyn interrupted.

Ruth knew her sister was right; she really did need a break. She hung her choring apron over the back of a chair and opened the door. "Where is this quiet place you're taking me to?"

Marilyn wiggled her eyebrows. "Remember how much fun we used to have when we were girls and went swimming in the neighbor's pond?"

Ruth's mouth fell open. "We're going swimming?"

Marilyn chuckled. "I think wading might be more appropriate for women our age. Or we can take off our shoes and let the tall grass tickle our toes as we listen to the birds sing and feel the wind blowing softly against our faces."

Ruth nodded, feeling a sense of excitement. She knew it would do her some good to get away for a while and let God minister to her tired soul.

If we aren't careful, the demands of life can overwhelm us. Taking the time to relax and enjoy the beauty of God's creation can restore and renew our tired bodies, as well as our minds.

In Matthew 11:28, God invites us to "Come unto me, all ye

that labour and are heavy laden, and I will give you rest." Even if you can't leave the house for a time of renewal, remember to pause several times during your busy day. Take a few deep breaths, close your eyes, and visualize yourself sitting in a quiet place beside the Lord.

FOOD FOR THOUGHT

It is not the load that breaks us down.
It's the way we carry it.

Tater Tots Casserole

Ingredients:

- 1 pound ground beef
- 4 cups canned or frozen mixed vegetables
- 1 can cream of mushroom soup
- 8 slices Velveeta cheese
- 3 cups tater tots

Preheat oven to 350 degrees. In a skillet, brown the ground beef and drain. Put the meat into a casserole dish. Put the mixed vegetables over the top of the meat, then pour the cream of mushroom soup over that. Top with Velveeta cheese, then add tater tots. Bake for 45 minutes to 1 hour.

CLARA MAST

BEFORE AND AFTER

I will instruct thee and teach thee in the way which thou shalt go:
I will guide thee with mine eye.
PSALM 32:8

"We've sure got a mess to clean up," Helen said to her husband, Abner. "Anyone who stops by our place today will wonder if it's been snowing during the month of *Yulei* [July]."

Abner glanced around the living room they had begun to remodel. "Jah, that insulation we've put in has gotten everywhere it's supposed to be and everywhere it's not supposed to be. This place is such a mess, it's hard to visualize how it used to look."

"But once it's cleaned up," Helen replied, "and the Sheetrock has been put in place, and the painting is done—think how nice it will be."

"You're right. With most remodeling jobs, it's necessary to make a mess before the job looks good," Abner said as he grabbed a broom and started sweeping the hunks of insulation littering the floor.

Helen nodded and reached for the other broom. "I think the same can be said for our own lives, don't you?"

Abner's eyebrows drew together. "What do you mean?"

"Sometimes we make a mess of things by making poor decisions. But hopefully, we learn from our mistakes."

"I've sure learned a lot from this remodeling project." Abner made a quick sweep with his broom. "It's important to know what you're doing so that the *after* looks better than the *before*. I'm glad

I had an instruction manual and help from family and friends to remodel this room."

Have there been times when you felt as if you had made a mess of something in your life? Maybe a hasty word was spoken in anger, a misunderstanding harmed a relationship with a friend, or you felt that because you had become idle in your Christian walk, everything seemed wrong.

God is always there to guide, direct, and help us through our mistakes. He can take our broken, messy lives and make them better than they were. By reading the Bible and following God's instruction manual, our lives are reshaped so we can become better than we were before.

FOOD FOR THOUGHT

People get into trouble when they think they can handle life without God.

FOOD FOR THE BODY

Tasty Amish Baked Chicken
Ingredients:
   2 cups finely crumbled crackers
   ¾ cup grated parmesan cheese
   2 teaspoons salt
   ¼ cup chopped parsley (if desired)
   ⅛ teaspoon pepper
   1 clove garlic, crushed, or 1 teaspoon garlic powder
   1 or 2 chicken fryers, cut up
   1 cup butter or margarine, melted

Preheat oven to 350 degrees. Mix first six ingredients. Dip pieces of chicken in butter, then in the crumb mixture, coating well. Arrange in an open pan. Pour remaining butter over all. Bake for 1 hour or until tender when poked with a fork.

MRS. JACOB STUTZMAN

Never Give Up

For our light affliction,
which is but for a moment,
worketh for us a far more exceeding
and eternal weight of glory.
2 Corinthians 4:17

As Elizabeth headed down the hall, she heard her two youngest children talking in the living room, where they had gone after supper.

"I give up! No matter how hard I try, I can't seem to sew this hunk of braided material without pricking my finger," Malinda complained.

"You should never give up," Eli said with a grunt. "Look at me. I've got two broken legs, and I can't walk right now, but I'm not giving up. I'll do whatever I'm able to do, even if I prick my finger a time or two. And once my legs have healed, I'll appreciate being able to walk again."

Elizabeth peeked into the living room. There sat Eli in his wheelchair, both legs elevated and encased in heavy casts. Yet, he wore a smile on his face. In his hands he held the braided throw rug he had been working on since he'd fallen from a tree a few weeks ago. Elizabeth had thought it might give him something to do during his recovery time. Eli had a determined spirit, and even though he couldn't run and play or do any of his regular chores right now, he'd made up his mind to do something useful while his legs mended. Not once since his mishap had she heard the boy complain or give in to depression. Even now, he set a good example to his younger sister.

There are times when everyone feels like giving up. It might be an illness, injury, family crisis, or fatigue that causes us to give in to depression or makes us want to quit.

During difficult times, our help should come from the Lord, for He has the remedy to all our problems. The next time you feel like giving up, try quoting this verse from Philippians 4:13 (NIV): "I can do everything through him who gives me strength."

FOOD FOR THOUGHT

Never say never, and never give up.

FOOD FOR THE BODY

Delicious Granola Bars
Ingredients:
2 (10 ounce) bags marshmallows (about 12 cups)
¾ cup butter
¼ cup honey
¼ cup peanut butter
5 cups oatmeal
4½ cups crispy rice cereal
1 cup coconut
1 package graham crackers, crushed
1 package chocolate chips (approximately 2 cups)

Put the marshmallows, butter, honey, and peanut butter in a saucepan. Heat until melted. Add the oatmeal, cereal, coconut, and graham crackers. Stir well. When the mixture cools slightly, add the chocolate chips and stir again. Pour into a 9 x 13-inch baking pan, cool completely, then cut into bars.

ESTHER RABER

LIFE IS A WALK

For we walk by faith, not by sight.
2 CORINTHIANS 5:7

Andy and Lorrie had just returned from a trip to town. The roads, still slick with snow in many places, had been hard to navigate, and Lorrie was glad they'd made it home safely.

Andy helped his wife down from their buggy and was about to unhitch the horse when he pointed to the field across from them. "Would you look at that? Herman's out there plowing with patches of snow still on the ground."

Lorrie's gaze went to their neighbor's field. Sure enough, Herman's four mules, though walking slowly, were helping him plow the snow into the dirt. Up and down the field they went with the plow, turning the snow under so it became one with the earth.

"My daed used to say that to plow under a warm snow is as good as plowing under a coat of manure," Lorrie said. "Do you suppose that's the thought Herman has in mind?"

Andy shrugged. "Maybe so. He's always had good crops before, and it's likely he'll have an even better one this year because he's forging ahead rather than complaining about the late snow we've had or sitting around idly waiting for it to melt. Even though it's plenty cold out, Herman is stepping out in faith and hoping the snow will help his field become healthier than it was before."

Each day of our lives we take steps through the choices we make. Some are baby steps; others are giant steps. The steps we take today determine our tomorrows. The Christian walk is a struggle from the beginning to the end because we must deal with the troubles we encounter in this world. Despite discouragements and difficult problems, it's important for us to forge ahead and keep walking with Jesus.

Colossians 1:10 reminds us, "That ye might walk worthy of the Lord unto all pleasing, being fruitful in every good work, and increasing in the knowledge of God."

FOOD FOR THOUGHT

Trust God to move your mountain, but keep on digging.

FOOD FOR THE BODY

Toasty Pecan Pie

Ingredients:

    1 cup light corn syrup
    ½ cup sugar
    3 eggs
    1 teaspoon vanilla
    ¼ teaspoon salt
    1 cup pecans
    1 pie shell, uncooked

Preheat oven to 350 degrees. Combine the syrup, sugar, eggs, vanilla, and salt in a bowl. Mix well. Add the pecans and stir to distribute the nuts. Pour into an unbaked pie shell and bake for 50 minutes or until done.

CLARA MAST

MISREAD DIRECTIONS

Trust in the LORD with all thine heart;
and lean not unto thine own understanding.
In all thy ways acknowledge him,
and he shall direct thy paths.
PROVERBS 3:5–6

Could you get me six dozen eggs?" Edna asked her friend Lucy. "I'll start mixing the eggs and breadcrumbs for the filling, while you chop onions and celery." The two young women had gotten together to prepare a number of chickens for their friend Ella's upcoming wedding.

"Are you sure the recipe calls for that many eggs?" Lucy questioned as she headed to the refrigerator.

"I don't want to take the time to read the recipe again, but I'm certain that's what it said."

Lucy shrugged. "Roasted chickens wouldn't be the same without the stuffing, would they?"

"I should say not." Edna opened the first carton of eggs her friend had placed on the cupboard. "This is kind of fun," she said, as she cracked eggs into a hefty enamel bowl. "Cooking together gives us a chance to catch up on our visiting."

Lucy nodded. Ever since she had arrived at Edna's, they'd been talking nonstop.

"It's a good thing the chocolate cake my mamm plans to make later today doesn't require any eggs, because there won't be any left by the time we're done here," Edna said.

Edna had just started on the last carton of eggs, when Lucy stopped chopping onions and squinted. "You sure that recipe calls for six dozen eggs?"

Edna reached for the index card lying on the cupboard. "Uh-oh."

"What's wrong?"

"Guess I should have taken the time to reread the directions instead of being in such a hurry to get the job done." Edna picked up the card and handed it to her friend.

Lucy's mouth dropped open. "It says we're supposed to use *three* dozen eggs, not six dozen."

"Oops." Edna covered her mouth with the palm of her hand and snickered. "Guess I'd better add a lot more bread crumbs so the filling won't be too moist."

Like Lucy and Edna, we can sometimes misread instructions when we become distracted or are in a hurry. The Bible is an instruction manual that must be carefully, thoughtfully, and prayerfully read in order to understand the direction God wants us to take in our daily walk with Him.

If we lean on our own understanding rather than following God's directions, we could make a mess of things. If we read the Bible and follow God's guidelines, everything will work out in the end.

*It's impossible to drive in the wrong direction
and arrive at the right destination.*

FOOD FOR THE BODY

Eggless Chocolate Cake
Ingredients:
>   2 cups brown sugar
>   ¼ cup lard or margarine
>   ½ cup cocoa
>   2 cups flour
>   1 teaspoon buttermilk
>   2 teaspoons baking soda
>   ½ cup boiling water

Preheat oven to 350 degrees. In a large bowl, mix all the ingredients thoroughly, adding the baking soda and water last. Pour into a 9 x 9-inch square baking pan and bake for 45 minutes or until done.

MRS. JOHNNY YODER

IMAGINATION

A man's heart deviseth his way:
but the LORD directeth his steps.
PROVERBS 16:9

When Joan heard the back door open, she turned from the stove where she had been making a pot of stew. She smiled as her husband, Luke, and teenage son, Stephen, stepped into the kitchen. "How'd it go in the woods today? Did either of you get a deer?"

Luke shook his head and hung his hunting jacket on a wall peg near the door.

"Thanks to our son's overactive imagination, we almost got ourselves some other critter, though."

"What was that?"

Stephen gave his mother a sheepish grin and flopped into a chair at the table. "*Ach*, it was nothin'."

Luke took the chair opposite their oldest boy. "Go ahead, son. Tell your mamm what happened out there."

"It was startin' to get dark, and I heard some leaves rustle in the bushes behind me," Stephen began. "So I whirled around, and sure enough, I could see the white of a deer's tail." He reached up and scratched the side of his blond head. "With a little imagination,

169

I could almost see the deer's profile."

"Then what happened?" Joan asked as she took a seat at the table.

"Then he fired the gun," Luke said before Stephen could reply. "And when he got no action, he reloaded and fired again."

"In the meantime, the critter's tail moved enough so I could see it was really a skunk and not a deer." Stephen's face turned red. "Lucky for me and Papa, that the old skunk didn't spray us."

Joan clasped her son's shoulder, trying not to laugh. "Guess it doesn't pay to rely solely on one's imagination, does it?"

He shook his head. "From now on I'm only gonna shoot when I can see clearly what I'm shootin' at."

Have you ever imagined something that wasn't there? Maybe you wanted something so much that you convinced yourself it was good for you without consulting God first. In our Christian lives, we must keep our focus on God and let Him direct our steps, rather than taking matters into our own hands or letting our imaginations run wild. He knows for certain what we can only imagine.

Second Timothy 2:7 reminds us, "Consider what I say; and the Lord give thee understanding in all things."

FOOD FOR THOUGHT

*The things I can see help me trust
God for the things I cannot see.*

FOOD FOR THE BODY

Tangy Vegetable Dip
Ingredients:
    1 (8 ounce) package cream cheese, softened
    ½ cup Miracle Whip
    1 egg, hard-boiled, mashed
    1 small onion, chopped
    1 teaspoon parsley
    1 teaspoon garlic salt
    ½ pint sour cream
    1 package onion soup mix
    Dash of pepper

In a mixing bowl, combine the above ingredients and mix well.
Serve with crackers or sliced fresh vegetables.

ESTHER RABER

HAPPY ENDINGS

The angel of the LORD encampeth
round about them that fear him,
and delivereth them.

PSALM 34:7

"Are you sure you don't mind taking the kinner to school today?" Milo asked as Winnie climbed into the buggy after her three girls had taken their seats.

"It's fine," Winnie assured her husband. "You have lots to do in the harness shop this morning, and since I'm not so busy today, I'm happy to take them."

"Be careful," he warned. "The roads could be slick from all the rain we've had this week."

"I'll be cautious."

Soon Winnie had the horse heading down the highway toward the one-room schoolhouse her daughters Regina, Mary, and Elma attended. Things went along well, and she was pleased to discover that the roads weren't slippery.

A short time later, she guided the horse into the schoolyard, and the girls climbed down from the buggy. "See you after school, Mama," Mary said.

Winnie waved. "Have a good day, you three."

"You, too, Mama," Regina and Elma said in unison.

Winnie watched her daughters head into the schoolhouse; then she picked up the reins and got the horse moving. She was about to leave the parking lot when the main bolt holding the buggy to the front axle snapped off. The horse took off with the front wheels and shaft dragging behind him.

"*Absatz* [stop]!" Winnie shouted.

The horse kept running.

Schoolteacher Rosemary and all her pupils ran outside to see what had happened. "Are you all right, Winnie?" Rosemary asked, leaning into the broken buggy.

"I'm fine. Just a little shook up is all."

"If that had happened when you were out on the main road, there could have been an accident."

Winnie nodded. There had been several buggy accidents in their community lately, and some had caused serious injuries. She knew God had protected her this morning.

Danger is an inevitable part of living, and God's provision doesn't always come with the removal of dangers. However, the presence of the Shepherd should help banish our fears. Life's most strengthening experience is the awareness of God's presence in our lives, no matter what difficulties come our way.

The apostle Paul, in 1 Corinthians 1:9, reminds us, "God is faithful, by whom ye were called unto the fellowship of his Son Jesus Christ our Lord."

Let's remember to thank God every day for His faithfulness.

FOOD FOR THOUGHT

Keep looking up,
for God is looking down.

FOOD FOR THE BODY

Raisin Cream Pie
Ingredients:
- 2 cups milk
- 1 cup sugar
- 2 egg yolks
- 4 tablespoons flour
- 1 cup raisins, cooked and drained
- 4 tablespoons butter
- 2 pie shells, baked

Put the milk in a saucepan and bring it to a slow boil. Add sugar, egg yolks, and flour. Cook until it thickens. Mix in the raisins and butter. Pour into two baked pie shells and let set.

LIZZIE MILLER

LOST AND FOUND

*I am with you always,
even unto the end of the world.*
MATTHEW 28:20

Doris and her family had just started up the road on their way to the home where church would be held, when their horse stumbled and fell.

Doris's husband, Fred, got out of the buggy and went around front to examine the horse. A few minutes later he returned. "I'm afraid our horse will never make it," he said with a shake of his head. "I should have put him out to pasture weeks ago."

Feeling a bit woozy from the intense heat of summer, Doris climbed down from the buggy and instructed their two young children to do the same.

"How are we going to get to church, Papa?" their daughter Selma asked.

"I guess you, Effie, and your mamm will have to walk. I'll lead the horse home and meet you there later."

Doris moved away from the buggy. She'd only taken a few steps when another horse and buggy pulled alongside of them.

"Need some help?" their friend Daniel called.

"Could you and Gladys give my wife and daughters a lift to church?" Fred asked. "I've got a worn-out horse on my hands and need to get him home."

"Sure, I can do that," Daniel responded.

When they arrived at Ben and Iris's place, where church was to be held, Doris stepped down from their friend's buggy, and so did Selma. Doris waited for her youngest daughter to exit the buggy, but there was no sign of Effie. She leaned inside, feeling befuddled. "Where's Effie?"

Selma covered her mouth. "*Ach*—oh, my! I think my little sister might be lost."

Doris drew in a shaky breath. "I thought both of you girls had gotten into Daniel's buggy."

"Maybe Effie's still in your buggy or with Fred," Gladys suggested.

"I can't believe I left without knowing my little girl wasn't with me."

Gladys gave Doris's shoulder a gentle squeeze. "You were upset about the horse and not thinking straight."

"We'll go back and see if we can find her," Daniel said.

A short time later, Doris found Effie asleep in the back seat of their buggy. Fred had managed to get the horse on his feet and had obviously taken him home, not realizing that their youngest child was still in the buggy.

"I'm glad you've been found," Doris murmured as she cradled her daughter in her arms.

Effie looked at her mother and said, "Was I lost?"

Every mother who has ever thought her child was lost knows

how Doris must have felt when she realized her little girl was missing. It's comforting to know that our heavenly Father always knows where His children are, even when we don't know we are lost. God will guide, direct, and help us find our way back to Him. All we need to do is call on His name.

In John 10:27, Jesus said, "My sheep hear my voice, and I know them, and they follow me." Even during the most distressing times, the Good Shepherd watches over His people and is always with us.

FOOD FOR THOUGHT

Life without Christ is a hopeless end.
With Christ it's an endless hope.

FOOD FOR THE BODY

Rhubarb Cream Delight

Ingredients for topping:
- 4 egg whites
- ¼ cup sugar

Ingredients for crust:
- 1½ cups flour
- ¾ cup oleo or margarine
- 3 tablespoons sugar

Ingredients for filling:
- 2 cups sugar
- ⅔ cup cream
- 4 cups chopped rhubarb
- 3 tablespoons flour
- 4 egg yolks, beaten

Preheat oven to 350 degrees. Beat the egg whites and sugar in a small bowl and set aside. Make the pie crust using the listed ingredients and press into a 13 x 9-inch pan. Bake for 20 minutes. In a kettle, combine filling ingredients and cook until thickened. Stir constantly. Pour hot filling onto baked crust. Top with the egg white mixture and brown the topping in the oven.

MIRIAM MILLER

TWISTS AND TURNS

Why are you downcast, O my soul?
Why so disturbed within me?
Put your hope in God, for I will yet praise him,
my Savior and my God.
PSALM 42:5–6 NIV

I'm so excited to be here," Mandie said to her friend Amelia as the teenage girls prepared to play a game of volleyball with the others who had come for the youth picnic.

"Jah, this is your first time, and I'm sure you'll have lots of fun," Amelia replied.

Soon the net was set up and the game had begun. Mandie did well getting the ball over the net, and she even scored a few points for her team. Then someone stopped the game so the net could be tightened. But after a few firm tugs on one of the poles, it popped out of the ground, hitting Mandie in the head.

That kind of hurts, she thought at first. Then she discovered blood dripping down her face and knew immediately that it was more than a scratch.

"Looks like that cut is going to need stitches," one of the boys said as he looked at Mandie's forehead. "Guess we'd better get someone to drive you into town so you can get that taken care of."

Mandie felt let down that she would have to leave the picnic, but she took comfort in knowing there would be other young people's gatherings.

A short time later, Mandie found herself in the emergency room with seven stitches and a large bandage on her head. "This wasn't the way I expected my first *yuchend* [youth] picnic to turn out," she told her parents, who had met her at the hospital, concern etching their faces. "I wasn't happy about having to leave early, but I'm glad my friends cared enough to see that I got help for my cut."

"Life is full of unexpected twists and turns," her mother said, putting her arms around her daughter. "It's how we learn to deal with our disappointments that matters."

Mandie's father patted her shoulder. "Your mamm and I are glad you weren't seriously hurt, and we're pleased that you're dealing with this so well."

Life is full of setbacks and disappointments, but giving in to negative thoughts or sinking into despair when things don't go our way won't change our circumstances. In the forty-second Psalm, when David struggled with discouragement, he reminded himself not to be discouraged because he knew that his hope was in the Lord.

If we keep our eyes on our heavenly Father, distressing, discouraging thoughts will lessen. The next time we're faced with one of life's disappointments, we can say with the psalmist, "Why are you downcast, O my soul?"

Remedy for discouragement: Reach up as far as you can, and God will reach down the rest of the way.

FOOD FOR THE BODY

Corn Salad

Ingredients:

    2 heads cabbage, shredded

    2 dozen ears sweet corn, kernels cut from the cob

    1 pint chopped carrots

    1 pint chopped celery

    1 pint navy beans

    2 red peppers, chopped

    2 yellow peppers, chopped

    3 cups sugar

    1 tablespoon celery seed

1 tablespoon salt
½ quart vinegar
2 quarts water

Mix the above ingredients together in a large pan, then pack into clean canning jars. Seal tightly and process in a pressure cooker for 30 minutes.

Mrs. William Miller

FINISHED WORK

For ye have need of patience, that,
after ye have done the will of God,
ye might receive the promise.
HEBREWS 10:36

All this foul weather we've had these last few weeks has made everything in the garden ripen too slowly," Alberta complained to her husband one morning as they stood on their back porch, watching the rain pelt the ground like a herd of stampeding horses.

Ezra reached for her hand and gave it a gentle squeeze. "We must have patience. The rain won't last forever. Sooner or later we'll have our crops."

She sighed. "I'm trying to be patient, but it's hard to wait—especially for something we need."

He nodded. "It's never easy to have patience, but if we fret because things don't happen when we want them to, we'll make ourselves miserable."

"You're right," Alberta agreed. "I'll try to have more patience."

The following week, the rain finally abated, and three weeks later than usual, Alberta's family had fresh corn and tomatoes to pick. On the evening of the first picking, Alberta, Ezra, and their six children gathered around the table to enjoy a taste of the garden.

Alberta placed a bowl of tender corn on the table. "I think it was worth the wait, don't you?"

"Jah, and we should thank the Lord for such a bountiful supply," her husband said.

Everyone nodded in agreement, and all heads bowed for silent prayer.

We live in a day of impatience. We want *instant* everything. Patience is said to be a vital part of the uniform of the true disciple of Christ. "Therefore, as God's chosen people, holy and dearly loved, clothe yourselves with compassion, kindness, humility, gentleness and patience" (Colossians 3:12 NIV).

God doesn't want us to lose faith or give way to despair. He wants us to press on with patience, always hoping for the best, always trusting Him.

FOOD FOR THOUGHT

Patience is a word that carries a lot of wait.

FOOD FOR THE BODY

Silver Cake
Ingredients:
> 1½ cups butter or shortening, softened
> 2 cups sugar
> 3½ cups flour
> 4 teaspoons baking powder
> Pinch of salt
> 1¼ cups milk
> ½ teaspoon vanilla
> 4 egg whites

Preheat oven to 325 degrees. Cream the butter and sugar in a bowl. In a separate bowl, sift the flour with the baking powder and salt. Add the sifted ingredients to the butter and sugar, alternating with milk and vanilla. Mix well. Beat egg whites until stiff, then fold into the mixture. Pour evenly into a large tube pan and bake for about 50 minutes.

MRS. ELI YODER

EVER FAITHFUL

*He that is faithful in that which
is least is faithful also in much.*
LUKE 16:10

Simon stepped into the barn, prepared to groom his horses. He had just picked up a currycomb when he noticed his ten-year-old son playing in the hayloft. "I could use some help," he called to the boy.

Ray scampered down the ladder and hurried into the stall, just as Simon was about to brush their horse, Tim, a sturdy Belgian.

"How old is Tim?" Ray asked as he grabbed another brush and began to groom the horse's long black tail.

"He's twenty-five years old," Simon replied. "Your mamm and I bought him soon after we were married, and he's been a faithful worker for us."

The horse neighed, as if in agreement.

Ray pursed his lips. "Twenty-five is kind of old for a work-horse, wouldn't you say?"

"Jah, but Tim doesn't work much anymore."

"Then why do you keep him?"

"Because he was a faithful worker for many years. In all the time we've had Tim, he's never refused to work, even when it's been obvious that he was tired." Simon patted the horse's flanks, and the animal whinnied in response. "Now that Tim is old and can't do so much, I've decided to reward his faithfulness by caring for his needs and allowing him to take life easy."

"Is that why you grind up his *hoi* [hay], so he can eat it better?"

Simon nodded. "That's right, and as soon as we finish grooming the horses, I'll reward your faithfulness with a bowl of your mamm's blackberry cobbler. How's that sound?"

Ray gave his father a toothy grin. "Sounds good to me."

Galatians 5:22–23 (NIV) reminds us: "But the fruit of the Spirit is love, joy, peace, patience, kindness, goodness, *faithfulness*, gentleness and self-control" (emphasis added). God wants us to serve Him and remain faithful until the end of our lives. When we face difficulties and hardships, He will give us the faith and strength to overcome the world. Some day, when we meet Him face-to-face, we will receive our reward for faithfulness.

FOOD FOR THOUGHT

Blessed are those who give without remembering and receive without forgetting.

FOOD FOR THE BODY

Blackberry Cobbler
Ingredients:
- 1 quart blackberries, cleaned
- ½ teaspoon salt
- 1 cup milk
- 2 teaspoons baking powder
- 6 tablespoons margarine
- 2 cups pastry flour
- 3½ cups sugar, divided
- 2 tablespoons cornstarch
- 1⅓ cups boiling water

Preheat oven to 350 degrees. Spread berries in the bottom of a 9 x 13-inch pan. In a large bowl, combine salt, milk, baking powder, margarine, flour, and 1½ cups sugar. Mix and sprinkle over the fruit in the baking pan. In another bowl, combine remaining 2 cups of sugar and cornstarch. Pour over the flour mixture. Then pour boiling water over all. Bake for 45 minutes.

LIZZIE MILLER

THE GOOD OLD DAYS

*To every thing there is a season, and a
time to every purpose under the heaven.*
ECCLESIASTES 3:1

This is going to take some getting used to," Mary Alice said to her husband, Mose, as they entered their new home.

With the help of several family members, a *daadihaus* [grandfather's house] had been built next door to their son's place so Henry could have the larger home for his growing family. Mary Alice and Mose's children were grown and had families of their own, and the small daadihaus would be adequate for their needs, keeping them close to family in case there was a need.

Mose glanced around the living room, which was much smaller than the one where they'd spent many hours with their children during their growing-up years. "It's going to be awfully quiet with just the two of us living here."

Mary Alice eased into the rocking chair—the same one she had rocked all ten of their children in when they were little. "I'm already missing the good old days," she said with a sigh. "Remember when Abner was born and you made this rocker so I could lull him to sleep whenever he got fussy?"

Mose nodded and took a seat on the sofa across from her. He folded his arms and leaned his head against the cushions. "It's a good thing to have fond memories, but if we're going to be happy living here, we need to look to the future rather than focusing on the past."

"You're right," Mary Alice agreed. "Instead of feeling sorry for myself because life isn't the same as it used to be, I'm going to purposely concentrate on making new memories in this daadihaus." She smiled. "We have much to be thankful for—good health, minds that are still pretty sharp, a loving family, and a heavenly Father who cares about our needs. We can spend the rest of our lives looking to the future, as we commit each new day to Him."

Everyone has a tendency to look back at the past or wish they could bring the good old days to life again. The past isn't really dead when it has provided us with the opportunity to establish relationships that can influence and bless our lives, as well as the lives of those around us.

It's all right to remember and treasure things from the past, but God wants us to enjoy each new day and to live it to the fullest, with gratitude.

FOOD FOR THOUGHT

*It is better to look back and prepare
than to look back and despair.*

Banana Cake

Ingredients:

    1⅔ cups sugar

    2⅓ cups flour

    1¼ teaspoons baking powder

    1 teaspoon baking soda

    1 teaspoon salt

    ⅔ cup shortening

    ⅔ cup buttermilk or sour milk

    1¼ cups mashed bananas

    2 eggs

    1 teaspoon vanilla

    ½ cup chopped nuts

Preheat oven to 350 degrees. Sift the dry ingredients together in a bowl; add the shortening, buttermilk, and bananas. Beat for 2 minutes, then add the eggs, vanilla, and nuts. Bake in 2 greased and floured 8 x 1½-inch round cake pans for 30–35 minutes. Cool and frost with your favorite frosting or whipped cream.

MRS. ELI YODER

CLOSE ATTENTION

This book of the law shall not depart out of thy mouth;
but thou shalt meditate therein day and night, that
thou mayest observe to do according to all that is
written therein: for then thou shalt make thy way
prosperous, and then thou shalt have good success.
JOSHUA 1:8

Jonas took a seat on the bleachers and squinted against the sun's glare. He and his son, Abe, had come to their community auction, and Jonas had his eye on a small table he wanted. It was made of mahogany and reminded him of one his folks had owned when he was a boy.

"Sure is a warm day," Abe said, removing his straw hat and fanning his face with it.

Jonas nodded. "I'm already thirsty."

"Want me to get us something cold to drink?"

"That would be nice."

Abe left the bleachers and headed into the area where vendors sold food and beverages.

With one eye on the table, which the auctioneer had said would be up for bid next, Jonas sniffed the tantalizing aroma of simmering hot dogs wafting through the air. His stomach rumbled, and he realized it was nearly noon. *I should have asked Abe to get us some food, as well as the cold drink.* He glanced at the concession stand where his son stood, hoping to catch his attention. But Abe was busy talking to the man selling root beer, and he never looked Jonas's way.

When the auctioneer hollered, "Who'll give me twenty dollars for this fine item?" Jonas snapped his attention back to the platform. He lifted the piece of cardboard with his number written on it and waited to see if anyone would bid against him.

Two more people placed their bids, and the price jumped to fifty dollars. The auctioneer asked if there were any further bids, so Jonas lifted his number once again, indicating that he would pay seventy-five dollars. He was pleased when the auctioneer shouted, "Sold for seventy-five dollars! What a good deal you got on this fine bicycle."

Jonas's mouth dropped open as he watched one of the auctioneer's assistants push a green bicycle off the platform. That's when Jonas realized he hadn't been paying attention. He had missed out on the item he'd wanted and ended up with something he had no use for. He would put the bike up for auction again, and he wouldn't be going home with a table today. He would, however, pay closer attention the next time he went to an auction.

The world has many things that can divert our attention away from God. A Christian's aim should be to magnify the Lord, but in order to do that we must pay close attention and heed the Father's will. Keeping our focus on God will help us make wise choices and keep us from being led astray. Daily prayer and Bible study will put our attention where it needs to be.

FOOD FOR THOUGHT

*A man seldom knows what he can do
until he tries to undo what he did.*

Cauliflower/Broccoli Salad

Ingredients for salad:

 1½ bunches broccoli, chopped

 2 heads cauliflower, chopped

 ½ pound bacon, fried and crumbled

 1 cup cheddar cheese, diced

Ingredients for dressing:

 1½ cups mayonnaise

 ½ cup sugar

 ⅓ cup vinegar

In a large bowl, combine the broccoli and cauliflower pieces. Add the bacon and cheese and mix well. In a separate bowl, combine dressing ingredients and mix well. Drizzle over salad and toss.

MATTIE STOLTZFUS

THE RIGHT TRACK

Two are better than one;
because they have a good reward for their labour.
For if they fall, the one will lift up his fellow:
but woe to him that is alone when he falleth;
for he hath not another to help him up.

ECCLESIASTES 4:9–10

Sadie glanced at the moon and the light that was reflecting against the glittering snow covering the ground. It was a beautiful night, and Sadie and her friends Carol and Irma had gone to a fellowship at a neighboring farm. A short time ago, they'd decided to leave the group for a while and take a walk in the woods.

Then Carol had announced that her hands were cold and said she was going back to the house to get her *hensching* [gloves].

"Do you want us to go with you?" Sadie asked.

Carol shook her head. "It's okay. I'll be all right on my own."

"Are you sure you can find your way back?" Irma asked.

"I'll be fine. You two keep walking. I'll catch up to you in a while."

Sometime later, when Carol had not returned, Sadie became worried. "Carol should have been here by now," she told Irma. "I'm afraid she might be lost in the woods."

Irma nodded. "She should have let us go with her."

"Carol! Carol!" Sadie called her friend's name over and over. When there was no response, she turned to Irma and said, "I think we should head back to the house and see if Carol is there. If she's not, we'll ask some of the others to help search for her."

"That's a good idea," Irma agreed.

A short time later, Sadie, Irma, and ten other young people combed the woods, searching for their missing friend, whom Sadie had learned had not even returned to the house to get her gloves.

With each step Sadie took, she prayed for her friend, until one of the boys finally shouted, "Here she is!"

Everyone rushed over to the tree where Carol and John stood. Carol was crying and shivering badly.

Sadie was glad they had thought to bring a blanket along. She wrapped it around Carol's shoulders and gave her a hug. "I'm relieved to know you're okay."

"I—I couldn't find my way back to the house," Carol sobbed. "I should have known better than to think I could go it alone in the woods on a cold, snowy night."

Like Carol, sometimes we, too, think we can go it alone. We like the feeling of independence, but there are times when we need others to help with things we're unable to do, or to help us overcome temptations.

In John 15:5 Jesus said, "I am the vine, ye are the branches: He that abideth in me, and I in him, the same bringeth forth much fruit: for without me ye can do nothing."

A tree needs more than one branch to be productive, and so do we. Jesus (the vine) should be our primary help, and the branches (others) are there to help us stay on the right track.

FOOD FOR THOUGHT

He who stands on his own strength will never stand.

Oatmeal Pie

Ingredients:

    ¼ cup butter or margarine
    ⅓ cup brown sugar
    2 large eggs
    1 cup Karo syrup
    ½ cup water
    ¾ cup quick-cooking oats
    ½ cup coconut
    1 pie shell, uncooked

Preheat oven to 350 degrees. Melt the butter. In a large bowl, blend sugar and eggs, stirring in butter slowly. Add Karo syrup, water, oats, and coconut, mixing well. Pour into an unbaked pie shell. Bake for 30–35 minutes or until done.

Mrs. Eli Yoder

THINK ON THESE THINGS

Finally, brethren, whatsoever things are true,
whatsoever things are honest, whatsoever things are just,
whatsoever things are pure, whatsoever things are lovely,
whatsoever things are of good report; if there be any virtue,
and if there be any praise, think on these things.
PHILIPPIANS 4:8

As Florence stepped onto the back porch to shake out her dust mop, a feeling of weariness washed over her like a drenching rain. It was a hot day, and she felt tired and grouchy from cleaning the house all morning. Having to deal with unexpected problems hadn't helped her disposition much, either.

Ever since she'd gotten out of bed, it seemed that nothing had gone right. First, she had dropped a carton of eggs on her clean kitchen floor. Then she'd cut her finger while slicing ham for breakfast. Next, she'd had to referee a disagreement between her two sons. After the meal was over and the older children had been sent off to school, Florence had taken a few minutes to read the newspaper, but that only succeeded in making her feel depressed. There were so many horrible things going on in the world, and it was hard to understand why God allowed such travesties.

A bird chirped from a nearby tree, drawing Florence's thoughts aside. She gazed into the yard at the profusion of blooming flowers and realized that there was always something positive to focus on.

Then Florence spotted her youngest daughter sitting under the maple tree, waving a bubble wand in the air and squealing with delight as the colorful bubbles floated into the air.

Florence joined Sally under the tree.

"Look at the pretty colors," the child said, smiling up at her mother.

Florence nodded and took a seat beside her precious little girl. "Would you mind sharing your bubble wand? I'd like to make some pretty colors, too."

If we habitually think destructive, negative thoughts, we will be pumping those thoughts into the world around us. As a result, others will be affected by our negative attitude. Looking on the brighter side of things—thinking constructive, pleasant, positive thoughts—can change lives by drawing positive results our way.

We are reminded in Proverbs 23:7, "For as he thinketh in his heart, so is he."

FOOD FOR THOUGHT

Every sunrise is a new message from God,
and every sunset His signature.

Turtle Cake

Ingredients:

    1 box chocolate cake mix
    1 (14 ounce) bag caramels
    ½ cup margarine
    ⅓ cup milk
    6 ounces chocolate chips
    6 ounces chopped nuts

Preheat oven to 350 degrees. In a large bowl, mix the cake mix as directed on the package and pour half into a greased 9 x 13-inch baking pan. Bake for 10–15 minutes. In a saucepan, melt the caramels, margarine, and milk. Pour caramel mixture on top of the cake, then pour the rest of the cake batter over the top. Bake another 20–25 minutes or until done. Sprinkle the chocolate chips and nuts on the top before it is completely baked.

CLARA MAST

Appreciation

In every thing give thanks: for this is the will of God in Christ Jesus concerning you.
1 Thessalonians 5:18

It was the last day of school, and Mildred, the schoolteacher, had mixed emotions. It was a sad day for her because it was the end of her teaching term at the one-room schoolhouse. It was also a happy day because she would be married in the fall.

Mildred had planned a program for the students' parents, followed by a picnic. During the program, several of the pupils gave recitations and sang a few songs. The parents showed their appreciation for their children's efforts, and Mildred could see by the smiles on her students' faces that they were having a good time.

At the close of the program, Mildred was getting ready to dismiss everyone to go outside for the picnic when Eunice and Cindy, two of the older girls, stepped forward. "This is from all of us," Eunice said, handing her teacher a gift.

Mildred placed the package on her desk and pulled the white tissue paper aside. A Friendship quilt was inside the box, and Cindy explained that each of the patches had been made, decorated, and signed by Mildred's students. Then the older girls and their mothers had met during a quilting bee to put the quilt together.

Mildred already owned several lovely quilts, but she knew this would be one of her most cherished possessions. "Danki," she said, smiling at everyone in the room. "I appreciate the hard work that went into this quilt, and most of all, I appreciate each of you."

All of us have had one or more special teachers from the past who stimulated us to grow and learn. Perhaps the teachers we appreciate most are those who have lived their lessons before us. They may have provided their pupils with a stimulus to faith and sacrificial giving.

When we give verbal expression for our appreciation, it makes us feel nearly as good as it does the one who receives the appreciation. How long has it been since you told someone you appreciate them? When was the last time you told God how much you appreciate Him?

FOOD FOR THOUGHT

If you can't be thankful for what you receive,
be thankful for what you escape.

Pineapple-Pudding Salad

Ingredients:

> 1 (16 ounce) can crushed pineapple, including the juice
>
> 1 (3 ounce) package instant pistachio pudding mix
>
> 1 (9 ounce) container Cool Whip
>
> 1 cup miniature marshmallows

In a large bowl, mix the pineapple and juice with the pistachio pudding mix. Add the Cool Whip and marshmallows. Mix well and refrigerate for several hours.

IDA KING

REAL BEAUTY

Favour is deceitful, and beauty is vain:
but a woman that feareth the LORD,
she shall be praised.
PROVERBS 31:30

Roselyn glanced at the calendar hanging on the kitchen wall. Thirty years ago today, she had married Lonnie. Tonight they would celebrate with their family by having dinner together. Roselyn took a seat at the table and poured herself a cup of tea as she reflected on her and Lonnie's first date. . . .

"I hope one of the boys will ask me to ride home in their courting buggy after the singing tonight," Roselyn whispered to her cousin Naomi as the girls rode in the back of Naomi's brother's open buggy on their way to the young people's gathering. Naomi was eighteen, and two years older than Roselyn. She'd already been to several singings and had told Roselyn that she'd ridden home with a couple of eligible young men at different times. This was Roselyn's first singing, and she was nervous.

"Do you have your eye on anyone in particular?" Naomi asked.

Roselyn dipped her head, feeling the heat of a blush cascade over her cheeks. "I'm kind of interested in Lonnie, but I'm not as *schee* [pretty] as some of the others girls who'll be there tonight, so he probably won't take notice of me."

"Real beauty comes from the inside; it's not our outward appearance," Naomi reminded. "My advice is to be yourself. The peaceful look I see in your eyes, and your friendly, dimpled smile, let me know that you have the love of God in your heart. That's what really matters. That's true inner beauty."

Roselyn brought her thoughts back to the present. Naomi had been right—Lonnie did think Roselyn was schee; he'd told her so many times over the years.

"As nice as it is to hear those sweet words from my husband," she murmured, "what really matters is how God sees me."

Nearly every woman wants to feel that she is pretty—especially to the man she loves. Real beauty isn't about wearing makeup, fancy clothes, or adornment, however. Real beauty comes from within. What makes us beautiful to God is when He sees us smiling, treating others kindly, and showing His love through our actions. What did you see when you looked in the mirror today? Was it your inner, real beauty?

FOOD FOR THOUGHT

Of all the things you wear, your
expression is the most important.

FOOD FOR THE BODY

Pot Pie

Ingredients for dough:

    2 eggs

    1 heaping tablespoon butter, softened

    2 cups flour

    ½ teaspoon salt

    ¼ cup milk

Ingredients for broth:

    2 or 3 cans chicken broth

    1 chicken, cut in pieces

In a bowl, beat the eggs well, then add remaining dough ingredients. Stir with a fork. If the dough doesn't mix right, add a little water. Roll the dough out thinly on a floured board. Cut into 2-inch squares. Set aside. Combine the chicken broth and chicken pieces in a large kettle and boil. Drop the dough squares into the boiling broth and cook on low heat for 1 to 1½ hours. For variety, pieces of beef and beef broth may be used instead of chicken.

RUTH STOLTZFUS

SWEET LIGHT

This then is the message which we have heard of him,
and declare unto you, that God is light,
and in him is no darkness at all.

1 John 1:5

As Marsha and her husband, Brad, pulled up to the small quilt shop, Marsha noticed a young Amish woman outside, hanging clothes on the line.

"If you'd like to go into the shop, I'll be right there," the woman called.

Brad opened the door, and as they stepped inside the quilt shop, shadows of darkness shrouded the room, making it difficult to see. "It's so dark in here," Marsha said. "I'll never be able to tell what the quilts look like without any light."

A few seconds later, the Amish woman entered the shop and turned on the gas lamps. "Feel free to look around. I'll be happy to answer any questions you might have," she told the English couple.

"Oh!" Marsha gasped. "Look at all the quilts and pillows; there are so many to choose from. Until you turned on the lights, I had no idea they were so beautiful." She pointed to a queen-size quilt sewn in muted blue and white colors. "I think I'd like to purchase this one."

The Amish woman lifted the quilt from the rack. "I especially like this pattern. It's the Colonial Star, and it's pieced in a series of blocks. The stars have been quilted around the diamonds, making a puffy, raised look, and causing them to stand out like flickering stars on a clear night."

The woman rung up the couple's purchase on her battery-operated cash register, and Marsha, pleased that they had stopped at the quilt shop, knew she would treasure her lovely quilt for many years.

Just as the beauty of the quilts was hidden from view until the gas lamps were turned on, others can't see Jesus until we let our light shine for Him. God gave us the sun, moon, and stars that we may see the beauty of His creation, and He, being light Himself, guides and directs those who follow Him, as we direct others to Jesus, the sweetest light of all.

"Truly the light is sweet, and a pleasant thing it is for the eyes to behold the sun" (Ecclesiastes 11:7).

FOOD FOR THOUGHT

As a bright sunbeam comes into every window,
so comes a love born of God's care for every need.

Food for the Body

Corn Ketchup
Ingredients:
- 1 dozen ears corn, kernels cut off cob
- 2 quarts ripe tomatoes or tomato juice
- 2 bunches celery, chopped
- 6 onions, chopped
- 1 cup vinegar (may be diluted with half water)
- 2½ cups sugar (may use less, if preferred)

Put all ingredients in a large kettle and boil for one hour. Pour into clean canning jars and seal. May be used like a salad.

Mrs. William Miller

A FINAL THOUGHT

It is my hope that after reading this devotional you may appreciate and understand the Amish culture a little better. Writing about the "plain people" fills my heart with joy and peace. Perhaps your heart has been touched in some special way or you have found a sense of direction that might help simplify your life.

Teach me thy way,
O LORD, and lead me in a plain path.
PSALM 27:11

Recipe Index

Scripture Index

ABOUT THE AUTHOR

WANDA E. BRUNSTETTER enjoys writing about the Amish because they live a peaceful, simple life. Wanda's interest in the Amish and other Plain communities began when she married her husband, Richard, who grew up in a Mennonite church in Pennsylvania. Wanda has made numerous trips to Lancaster County and has several friends and family members living near that area. She and her husband have also traveled to other parts of the country, meeting various Amish families and getting to know them personally. She hopes her readers will learn to love the wonderful Amish people as much as she does.

Wanda and her husband have been married over forty years. They have two grown children and six grandchildren. In her spare time, Wanda enjoys photography, ventriloquism, gardening, reading, stamping, and having fun with her family.

Wanda has written several novels, novellas, stories, articles, poems, and puppet scripts.

Visit Wanda's Web site at www.wandabrunstetter.com and feel free to e-mail her at wanda@wandabrunstetter.com.